Blue Skies Guide

The 25 Best Day Walks in Hong Kong

Blue Skies Guide

The 25 Best Day Walks in Hong Kong

Martin Williams

JOHN BEAUFOY PUBLISHING

Reprinted in 2023

First published in the United Kingdom in 2018 by John Beaufoy Publishing Ltd
11 Blenheim Court, 316 Woodstock Road, Oxford OX2 7NS, England
www.johnbeaufoy.com

ISBN 978-1- 912081-76-9

Edited by Krystyna Mayer
Cartography by William Smuts
Project management by Rosemary Wilkinson
Designed by Gulmohur Press, New Delhi

Page 2: *Approaching rugged Ma On Shan from the east*

Printed and bound in Malaysia by Times Offset (M) Sdn. Bhd.

CONTENTS

Escaping the City 6

Further Information – and Conservation 156

Some Cantonese Words for Hong Kong Explorers 157

Acknowledgements 158

Index 159

Escaping the City

Ferry approaching Chi Ma Wan, Lantau

Hong Kong is renowned for its tightly packed high-rises; a thriving business centre, its city life surges along at a frenetic, stressful pace. Yet Hong Kong has a greener, more tranquil side: around 40 per cent of the land area is designated as country park – more, people say, than in any other territory.

Reaching the greener side is easy. Even the seemingly remote parts are seldom more than a couple of hours from the claustrophobic confines of the city. By combining journeys by car or public transport with walking, you can experience wild, rugged hills, forested valleys, reservoirs and waterfalls, temples and ageing villages, long-abandoned forts and near-uninhabited islands.

All feature in this book, which is based on articles I wrote (and photographed) for the *South China Morning Post*; most appeared in a column called 'A day away'. These became *Hong Kong Pathfinder*, which was enhanced in subsequent editions and has now undergone a major revamp – a reboot to appear with a new publisher and with a new title, *The 25 Best Day Walks in Hong Kong*. Mostly, the outings do not require a day of

hiking – there is typically plenty of time to take photos, admire views, find wildlife and smell the flowers.

This version of the book includes new chapters, omits some walks spoilt by development and features revised information, together with new maps and photos. The underlying principle remains the same: a presentation of a selection of routes that make for excellent outings.

You do not need fancy gear to follow the itineraries described here. Besides wearing suitable clothing and footwear, the main item to take, especially in summer, is something to drink.

A mobile phone can help in case of emergencies – along with checking the weather, taking photos, indicating compass directions, determining your location, helping you to follow your route on maps, serving as a torch if you find yourself finishing a hike in the dark, and more.

Each section of the book contains an itinerary suitable for a day's outing. Of course, you might cover part of a route, walk an extra length of trail or create your own combos with sections from different chapters, such as hiking from Lead Mine Pass above Shing Mun to Tai Po Kau, or taking a long weekend to do various routes on Lantau.

Particularly if you want to plan alternative routes, you may want to take a map with you. Maps in the Countryside Series produced by the Survey and Mapping Office are useful. They are available from Map Publications Centres, and some bookshops and websites (see page 156 for some other sources of information).

Dress to suit the weather and the conditions expected along the route. Even in summer, it is advisable to usually wear a long-sleeved shirt to guard against the sun. A spare shirt is useful to change into before returning to the city.

Trainers or sandals designed for hiking are adequate for walking, though walking boots give better ankle support. Whichever you buy, it may be worth choosing a pair that has soles with some 'give'; very hard plastic soles can skid on damp rocks. If rain seems possible, perhaps take a folding umbrella.

Also useful are sun cream, perhaps a swimming costume, a torch in case it is dark before you finish (torch apps on smartphones can work pretty well too), and mosquito repellent. Mosquitoes favour damp, shady places; few will bother you as you walk, but they can be a nuisance if you halt in woodland.

Depending on the route, you may wish to carry a picnic lunch. It is also important to carry something to drink. Drinking water or soft drinks is essential during summer, when dehydration is a risk. If you walk in summer, you may be surprised how much you need to drink; even 3 litres (5 pints) or more can be insufficient for a half day's hiking. So, unless your route is very short or well served by shops, take plenty; it is no fun becoming increasingly thirsty, with no water left and the next shop some distance away. A bottle of water and one of a sports drink is a good combination in summer, the sports drink helping to replace salts.

Autumn is the best season for walking; the days are often sunny, with pleasant temperatures and low or moderate humidity. Though the season is underway by September, temperatures may remain high well into October, and the most comfortable days are typically in November and December. Unfortunately, the air at this time tends to be sullied by pollution from across

the border, along with shipping and Hong Kong traffic, marring views. Even so, you will be in cleaner air than in the city; and there are clear spells, chiefly just after blustery winds have blown in from the north.

By late December the cold fronts that in autumn invariably bring clear, dry days may instead be followed by grey skies; with no sun, the days may be chilly, sometimes with drizzle. This grim weather is typical of January and February: as the north-east monsoon blows, temperatures may barely rise above 10° C. Yet although in some years this weather seems never-ending, there may be welcome sunny spells. By March, spring is beginning. The days are warmer while the nights may remain chilly, and fogs are common.

Hikers on Ma On Shan

April sees the last cool weather for months. There may also be an end to grey weather, although when it does rain showers are typically heavier than in winter. Especially later in the month, the days may be hot, with temperatures of around 30° C.

May and June are warm and humid, often with rainy spells – especially when the south-west monsoon of summer is blowing, or when there are tropical storms or typhoons. While these storms may bring deluges and strong winds (hurricane force if there is a direct hit by a typhoon), the weather while they build over the South China Sea is fine and hot. Because of the higher rainfall, these months can be good for visiting waterfalls. However, if you go walking, take it easy: the heat and humidity are energy sapping.

Temperatures peak in around the second half of July and first half of August. Walking is tough at this time, but the air can be wonderfully clear. Combined with lush summer greenery, the views can be stunning. Should you head out, maybe choose shorter routes and/or aim for higher places (such as around Ngong Ping on Lantau, where temperatures can be pleasant if there is a good breeze), be prepared to sweat a lot and be wary of heatstroke. Towards the end of August, early mornings are a bit cooler ('cooler' may mean 26–28° C at sunrise), as autumn begins.

Not surprisingly, few people walk the longer trails during summer. At other times of the year trails may be quiet on weekdays, but busy at weekends and during public holidays.

Night hiking has become popular in recent years, partly because in summer it affords a way of escaping the daytime heat. It certainly makes for a different experience in the Hong Kong countryside, with its own special rewards – including the chance to see nocturnal creatures such as fireflies, along with various frogs and snakes.

The Hong Kong Observatory's homepage at www.hko.gov.hk/contente.htm has information including the latest forecast and the (non-too-reliable) nine-day forecast, along with radar imagery. The related *MyObservatory* app is well worth installing on smartphones to take on hikes.

If you travel by public transport you will find that there is a great variety to choose from. The MTR (Mass Transit Railway) has stations from which you can take other transport to the countryside. To avoid crowded carriages on the MTR's East Rail, travel first class.

Grading system for walks

There is a simple grading system for the walks in this book, ranked on a scale of * to *****, based on notions of how challenging 'average' people might find the outings. Note that summer heat makes all outdoor activities more challenging, with the threat of dehydration or heatstroke. The walks are ranked as follows:

*   Easy strolling.
**   Similar to a stroll in a park.
***   Some uphill sections make for a little challenge.
**** Sustained uphill sections and perhaps quite lengthy.
***** Steep slopes to climb, perhaps via rough tracks, plus a fair distance.

Bear in mind that how hard people find the walks also depends on the individual. A woman I once met was in a group for 'easy' short hikes, but later said that the walk had been hard for her. I have puffed and panted slowly to the top of Ma On Shan, yet seen people almost bounce up – I recall one man in running gear doing this with just a small bottle of water, yet reacting as if he had barely climbed a flight of steps

There are also ferries, buses, minibuses (on all buses and green-striped minibuses, no change is given) and taxis. If your attempt at pronouncing a place name is not understood, show the driver the Chinese characters (as on the maps in this book) for your destination.

Octopus cards are stored-value cards that can be swiped in front of panels when entering and exiting MTR turnstiles and alighting on buses, and before queuing for first-class compartments on East Rail trains. They can be used on most forms of transport, and are highly convenient. You can buy them, and add value to them, at MTR stations, ferry terminals and other outlets.

Hong Kong is a fast-changing place; several of the localities described in this book may soon look very different – including the north coast of Lantau, where the formerly wild landscape is now dominated by a new town, and the new airport and associated transport links. Your comments, notes on changes to landscapes or routes, and suggestions would be very welcome. Write to Martin Williams, c/o John Beaufoy Publishing, or email martin@hkoutdoors.com, or message me via my Facebook page at www.facebook.com/docmartinhk.

Key to map symbols

●●●●　route of main walk

••••　route of supplementary walk

　　　town or village

●　　place of interest

　　　toilets

　　　small stores with drinks, and rural restaurants

Countryside and new town: Yuen Long, north-west Hong Kong

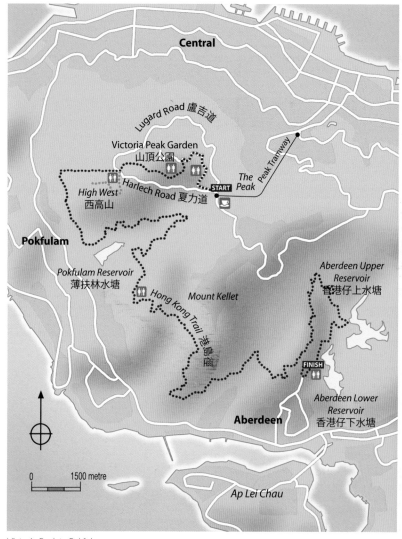

Lugard Road 盧吉道

Victoria Peak Garden
山頂公園

The Peak

Peak Tramway

START

High West
西高山

Harlech Road 夏力道

Pokfulam

Pokfulam Reservoir
薄扶林水塘

Mount Kellet

Hong Kong Trail 港島徑

Aberdeen Upper Reservoir
香港仔上水塘

FINISH

Aberdeen Lower Reservoir
香港仔下水塘

Aberdeen

0   1500 metre

Ap Lei Chau

Victoria Peak to Pokfulam

Peak to Pokfulam
The wild west

11.5km (7 miles) ***

After admiring classic views over Victoria Harbour, head into dense woodland and hike past reservoirs amid the rolling hillsides of south-west Hong Kong Island.

High West on a summer afternoon

At its start, by the upper Peak Tram station, Mount Austin Road looks as if it might be just another road to a residential district. However, along it are trees and open spaces, as well as apartment blocks, and soon after starting up the road, there is a bend with a view better than that from the tram station.

It is a familiar view to Hongkongers – across Central, Wanchai, Victoria Harbour and Kowloon – but also a chance to look over the changing cityscape.

Mount Austin Playground

Echoes of colonial times at Victoria Peak Gardens

The road wends further uphill, leaving the apartment blocks behind. On reaching Victoria Peak Gardens, there is a chance to drop down to the left and follow the Governor's Walk. The path crosses a stream and leads away from the manicured gardens, to curve around the hillside, to the other, wilder side of Hong Kong

The city now seems remote. There are no buildings by the path, just trees and shrubs. Woodland ripples across the hillside: many of the trees were planted to regulate water flowing to Pokfulam Reservoir in the valley below.

When you reach a junction there is a detour to the top of Victoria Peak Gardens and a viewpoint with an impressive vantage across the harbour, and west towards

Lantau, Cheung Chau and other islands. Then it is back down the steps, and on to where Lugard and Harlech Roads meet.

If you have energy to spare, there is a chance for a wonderful side excursion here, along a trail leading from behind a tiny park. Level at first, it climbs steps to the summit of High West, a superb viewpoint. The other trail from the summit is steep, so whenever I head up, I retrace my route from here to the park.

This outing continues by joining the Hong Kong Trail, which has wound around Lugard Road from its start at Peak Tram station. It leads westwards, along the north slopes of High West. After a rest area, the trail turns down and south.

The city is close again; there is the hum

of air-conditioners in Pokfulam high-rises that are almost level with the path. The trail enters woodland, and the high-rises are lost from view.

The path runs up and around to the left, and crosses streams cascading down to the reservoir. At the main stream the path turns sharp right, almost doubling back on itself as it hugs the valley contours.

There is another uphill section, then a valley overgrown with tall, dense grass. It was once surely cultivated; trees have yet to assert themselves. With a low ridge hiding Pokfulam, it seems a secret place.

Along this stretch of the trail there is little shade. On one hot day I soaked my shirt with water from a stream: air-conditioning for summer hikers.

Woodland again. That hot day, a squirrel shrieked in alarm, scampered higher in a tree, then sat and watched me pass. The path runs downhill, follows a formerly 'difficult' section now made easier by steps, and skirts a sharp spur to a hillside overlooking Aberdeen. This is a noisy place, with a continuous racket from traffic and construction work. The nearest buildings are only a couple of hundred metres away.

The path runs alongside a catchwater bound for Aberdeen Upper Reservoir. After curving to the right it crosses the

catchwater. A sign shows the Hong Kong Trail leading up a valley. Instead, turn right almost immediately, where arrows painted in red point up a flight of steps: a shortcut.

At a junction, more red arrows point upwards. The slope then eases. The shortcut ends at the Hong Kong Trail again; a right turn leads to a woodland trail.

Much as near Pokfulam Reservoir, this trail follows the contours of the hillside. Many trees here were also planted, to improve the watershed. However, nothing is regimented about these woods; wild plants thrive, including creepers in dense tangles beneath the canopy. If not for the sounds of Aberdeen, which soon fade, this path could be far from city life.

While the Hong Kong Trail continues eastwards – bound for Big Wave Bay – there is a chance to leave it where a signpost indicates a track to the right,

Greater Necklaced Laughingthrush

A stream tumbling towards Pokfulam Reservoir

Strolling and fishing on Aberdeen Upper Reservoir dam

Getting there

- The Peak Tram provides a popular way of reaching the upper tram station. There can be long queues for it, in which case perhaps consider taking a bus.
- From outside Aberdeen Country Park (on Aberdeen Reservoir Road), take a taxi, bus 7 (to Central) or 76 (Causeway Bay), or minibus 4A or 4C (Causeway Bay), or 4B (Wanchai). Take food and drink: a kiosk at the top of Victoria Peak Gardens is the only shop en route.

Notes

- The route is well signposted. The Countryside Series map *Hong Kong Island & Neighbouring Islands* is useful; from it, you can find many alternative routes. For instance, a route north from the Peak leads down through Lung Fu Shan Country Park, which has the remains of an old fort, Pinewood Battery, dating from 1903.

Wild Boar are 'tamer' nowadays

towards Aberdeen Reservoirs, 300m (985ft) away. It soon arrives by the upper reservoir, and there is a narrow road towards Aberdeen. At first it keeps to the catchwater, the route followed before the shortcut; it is wider here, swollen by waters from further tributaries.

You might spot Wild Boar here. I once saw three or four, which wandered across the road as if almost oblivious to people; a man who liked to play mahjong with friends at a table set in a lawn told of a male boar that liked to rest right beside them.

After turning left and going gently down, the road passes the Aberdeen Country Park visitor centre. I have been here before and thought that the centre's exhibits seemed dated, with some questionable information on wildlife. Still, the air-conditioning is pleasant.

Then you can go to Aberdeen's edge, and take a taxi or bus back to the city.

Summer flowers on High West

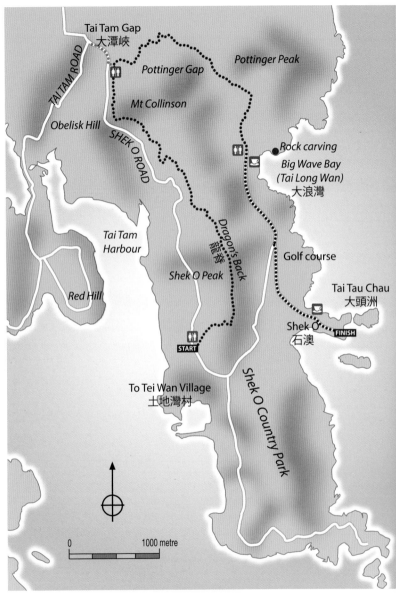

Tai Tam Gap
大潭峽

Pottinger Peak

TAI TAM ROAD

Pottinger Gap

Mt Collinson

Obelisk Hill

SHEK O ROAD

Rock carving

Big Wave Bay
(Tai Long Wan)
大浪灣

Tai Tam
Harbour

Dragon's Back
龍脊

Golf course

Red Hill

Shek O Peak

Tai Tau Chau
大頭洲

START

Shek O
石澳

FINISH

To Tei Wan Village
土地灣村

Shek O Country Park

0   1000 metre

Short trail, varied scenery – Dragon's Back on Hong Kong Island

Over Dragon's Back to Shek O
Squiggles on a rock face

10km (6 miles) **

Probably the best short hike in Hong Kong leads up and along Dragon's Back in southeastern Hong Kong Island, where the coast is also wonderfully scenic.

As the road winds its way up the ridge above Chai Wan, the city slips away. Soon there is woodland on both sides. There is a left turn, and a sign announcing 'Shek O Country Park'.

The road is narrow here, just wide enough for two lanes of traffic as it hugs the steep hillside, passing a small car park, then a tiny car park on the right. Soon after this there is a bus stop above the hamlet of To Tei Wan – the start of this outing. On the left is a noticeboard with a map: section

eight of the Hong Kong Trail starts here, and should take around 2¾ hours.

Stone steps lead uphill to the ridge called Dragon's Back. They pass the ruins of a small house, now hidden amid bamboo. A signpost points the way up the hillside, which on a quiet day seems to belong only to birds and a sprinkling of hikers. Soon the trail is on the exposed spine of the dragon.

Wind-pruned grasses and shrubs carpet the ridge. Below the steep eastern slope is Shek O: close enough to hear the sounds

A Dragon's Back sunset

Looking west from Dragon's Back, with Stanley just left of centre

of traffic, yet somehow remote from this hilltop trail. The gentler west slope runs down to Tai Tam Bay; across the water are Stanley, and a grim, faceless cluster of houses on Red Hill. Beyond them lie wooded hills and reservoirs.

The trail turns north, climbing the ridge to an even better vantage, atop the 284m (930ft) Shek O Peak. Then down, and up to another peak – where during easterly winds the slope can be a favourite launch point for paragliders – before dropping down and left, away from the ridge.

The sheltered west slopes of Dragon's Back are clothed in young forest. On spring days some of the trees are tinged red with new leaves, while others are brighter – greener – than their neighbours.

The trail levels off and meanders through the trees, crossing a stream where there are small but attractive cascades after wet weather. There is a junction where a narrow road meets the track, now itself concrete. The road passing through Tai Tam Gap is close by, offering an easier way to reach the trail here for anyone wanting to enjoy Dragon's Back, and to miss the less interesting trek down to Big Wave Bay.

The Hong Kong Trail now follows the access road, before turning off down steps to Big Wave Bay (Tai Long Wan). There is little of interest in either the walk or the views, but at least the bay is a good place to visit.

There are houses where mahjong sessions may be well underway, and fields and low buildings below the hillside. If you bring someone here who did not know the

place, they might guess they were in the darkest New Territories.

There is a small park, sometimes popular for barbecues. A shack offers food and drinks, and the menu of a shop facing the beach lists noodle dishes.

The sand is pale, the water blue – looking surprisingly clear and inviting to anyone. Due to the onshore winds, the waves are indeed big by Hong Kong standards, making this a hotspot for local surfers. There are showers here; even if you do not swim, you may find them useful after the hills.

A concrete path has been built to a rock carving on the bay's north headland. Ancient it might be, but I reckon only an archaeologist could be inspired by the carving – housed in its own shelter, it consists just of squiggles on a rock face.

Leaving Big Wave Bay, you can walk along the road towards Shek O. Big

Evening view of Shek O from Dragon's Back

driveways lead to big, fancy houses or mansions hidden among trees.

The road cuts between golf course fairways. The golf course is usually almost bereft of people, but is immaculately kept. This is not golf for the proletariat, as once forecast for the sport in Hong Kong, but for taipans and tai-tais.

Arriving at Shek O the first impression is of a roundabout, traffic, tourists and restaurants. The main road of the village leads eastwards from the roundabout. Traffic moves fitfully, squeezing between buildings, parked cars and strolling pedestrians. The road climbs a little to a low hilltop with expensive-looking housing. At the tip of the headland the road ends by a place with architecture modelled on old Chinese temples, or even the Forbidden City.

Scenic Shek O Beach

There are steps down, and a footbridge across to a small, rugged island – Tai Tau Chau. The concrete path builders have been here, too, easing the way to barbecue

Summer at Shek O Beach

sites. The top of the southern cliffs is a good place to sit, rest and savour the views of the east coast of Hong Kong Island, along with islands including Waglan – where a weather station records some of the most intense winds of typhoons impacting Hong Kong.

Going back to the headland, just below it is one of Hong Kong's best beaches.

In north Shek O there are ramshackle houses along narrow streets, and a small, old temple with paintings adorning the outer wall. Here you can still find yourself in a Hong Kong style coastal village, and perhaps walk along an alley to the popular Chinese-Thai restaurant next to the roundabout.

The bus station is a box-like, two-storey building with fading yellow walls; it would not look out of place in America's Midwest, the sort of place where the main excitement in a day is some tumbleweed rolling by. Built in 1955, it is listed as a grade two historic building, with architecture influenced by the Bauhaus style and Art Deco lettering on the balcony – and helps to make Shek O the most eccentric village in Hong Kong.

Getting there
- To reach the start of the route, take a minibus, taxi or bus no. 9 bound for Shek O, from near Shau Kei Wan MTR station, and get out above To Tei Wan.
- To join the route after the Dragon's Back section — or to walk Dragon's Back from north to south — get out just after the tiny roundabout at Tai Tam Gap. Look for a sign indicating 'Shek O Country Park', head up the flight of steps beside it, then up the road past a correctional institution. You will soon reach a board with a map covering the Hong Kong Trail; here, you can keep straight on to Big Wave Bay, or turn right to Dragon's Back.

Getting back
- Minibuses and bus no. 9 depart Shek O for Shau Kei Wan.

Notes
- Carry plenty of water or soft drinks: there are no stalls until Big Wave Bay. Especially for walking the Dragon's Back, wear footwear with a good grip.
- The trail is well marked. If you want to take a map, the best is the Countryside Series map *Hong Kong Island & Neighbouring Islands*.

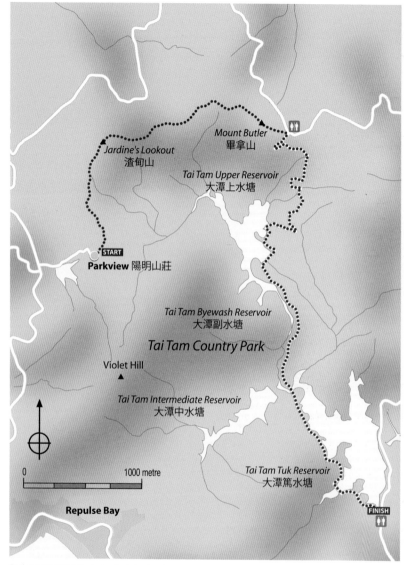

Parkview to Tai Tam via Jardine's Lookout

Parkview to Tai Tam
Vale of the reservoirs

12km (7½ miles) ****

Enjoy city views from hilltop lookouts, before dropping down through a broad wooded valley with picturesque reservoirs.

The city and Victoria Harbour from Jardine's Lookout

What an inglorious place Parkview is for starting a hike. Controversial when it was built – as it would spoil the scenery of Tai Tam Country Park – it looks like the kind of creation former Soviet planners might have come up with if asked to design a residential 'community' for affluent short- to medium-term stayers with no ties to the land. Happily, there is no need to linger here.

A flight of steps leads up a hillside to the north; here the Wilson and Hong Kong Trails run together. There is some woodland at first, but soon the path is heading up a hillside that is evidently struggling to recover from deforestation and erosion; it is mostly covered with shrubs and dotted with red pines. The path levels, and arrives at the top of Jardine's Lookout. The climb is rewarded with the kind of views that make this route special.

To the south and south-east are rolling hills, the Tai Tam reservoirs and Tai Tam Bay. At the end of a very short path to the north is a vantage overlooking Victoria Harbour.

Mount Butler view, with the city almost obscured by smog

Happy Valley and Causeway Bay are in the near distance, with the Kowloon peninsula beyond and the Kowloon hills as a fine backdrop to the city.

The trail drops down from Jardine's Lookout and a disused quarry comes into view on the left. Near it are radio antennae scattered over a hill, a building that looks like a disused warehouse combined with an apartment block, and beside this a road that disappears at the entrance to a tunnel into the hill, which looks to be guarded by an imposing gate with stout pillars. After reaching the bottom of the incline, the trail climbs steps close to the quarry. The view is wilder here and – while it is not crumbling just yet – at least Parkview is receding.

Then there is a gentle stretch, along which the Wilson Trail abruptly leaves and makes off for the northern New Territories. There follows a dip down a ridge, and a short uphill stretch where the trail tunnels up between dense trees and bamboo along stone slabs that could have been transplanted from an old New Territories trail, and reaches the top of another peak, Mount Butler.

This is a marvellous spot in which to rest and enjoy the scenery. Again, there are views over the city around Victoria Harbour on one side, while hills, reservoirs and sea dominate on the other.

The city views end here. The trail plunges down a steep flight of steps to Mount Parker Road, which is narrow, with access restricted to vehicles with permits. At the road a Hong Kong Trail sign points down towards the reservoirs. Almost immediately, the road is amid dense forest with no buildings in sight. The meandering road makes for easy and pleasant walking.

The road passes Tai Tam Upper Reservoir. This was the second reservoir built on Hong Kong Island, with construction lasting from 1883 to 1888, and its water supply helped the early development of the city that was then burgeoning on the north shore of the island. The dam now lies on the Tai Tam

Waterworks Heritage Trail, along with other dams of three later reservoirs, plus aqueducts, bridges and associated buildings.

A few minutes' walk beyond the dam, the Hong Kong Trail bears left. The stretch from here to Tai Tam Road is not very interesting, so is perhaps best avoided unless you want to follow it to near a small bridge, for a scramble down to the lovely Tai Tam Mound Waterfall.

There's a bridge across a broad creek, where three streams meet and feed into Tai Tam Tuk Reservoir. The road is almost dead level now, skirting the western shore of the reservoir. With forest to the right, reservoir on the left and hills beyond, this is in one of those places where Hong Kong city seems distant even though it is little more than a stone's throw away.

Getting there

- To reach the start of the walk, take bus 6 or 61 – they run from Exchange Square in Central – to Wong Nai Chung Gap, at the top of the incline from Happy Valley. Walk up towards the left, to an information board and the flight of steps towards Jardine's Lookout.
- At Tai Tam Road there are buses heading to near Shau Kei Wan MTR station (to the left as you approach the road), and towards Stanley – where there are shops, bars and restaurants, and a terminus for buses to the city.

Notes

- Take plenty to drink; there are no shops en route. The Countryside Series map *Hong Kong Island & Neighbouring Islands* is useful.

The road crosses a picturesque arched bridge, makes a final sweep past the mouth of an inlet and meets Tai Tam Road.

Tai Tam Tuk Reservoir Masonry Bridge, built with granite blocks in 1907

Po Toi 蒲台島

Rugged Trail

Tai Wan 大灣

Mo's Old House 巫氏廢宅

START FINISH

Wan Tsai

Pier

Ngong Chong

Buddah's Palm Cliff 佛手巖

Monk Rock

Nam Kok Tsui

0   400 metre

Trails on Po Toi

Po Toi
Small but perfectly formed

9km (5½ km) ***

Enjoy fine coastal hiking and scenery, and maybe some birdwatching, little more than a stone's throw from Hong Kong Island.

Though it lies just 3km (2 miles) off the south-eastern tip of Hong Kong Island, the island of Po Toi is one of those places that is easily overlooked when planning a rural outing. It is popular with junk parties – who gorge on seafood in restaurants set in a sheltered cove, and perhaps muster the energy for a waddle to a temple.

Boatloads of day-trippers arrive on Sundays and public holidays, and are frogmarched along trails past the main scenic spots. However, Po Toi deserves more attention, especially in summer, when the hiking here is just sufficient to be taxing in the heat, and there are days when you can appreciate the setting of this island and a host of others in the tropical South China Sea.

The public ferry trundles out past Stanley Fort and Beaufort Island, and rocks where fishermen sometimes lurk. It berths in Po Toi's main cove, on the western shore. In the 1960s, Po Toi was home to perhaps 1,000 people, most of whom lived around this cove.

The popular Ming Kee Seafood Restaurant, just a short walk from the pier

Drawn by the booming city and driven out by mainland China marauders, all but a handful have since left. There are ruined buildings among trees by the pier; others are scattered nearby, and many more must have long since vanished, smothered by shrubs and climbers.

A short way up from the pier, at a junction, is a run-down shop where, in winter, you can buy seaweed collected from the shoreline – it is reportedly good for a range of ailments. Turn right at the stall and the trail leads to another junction, marked by a wooden signpost.

A flight of concrete steps leads uphill from the signpost, towards the ridge above. The trail is sheltered at first, as it passes through dense young woodland. Then trees give way to scrub and grass, and there are views of the cove below. On the right a side trail leads to Old Mo's House – also known as the Ghost House, a ruined building in which Japanese soldiers stayed during the Second World War.

The concrete steps end and the trail appears to fizzle out – although it actually keeps climbing, mostly over bare rock. Then there are steps again, to a trail junction on top of the ridge. Here you can look east across the rolling granite hills of the island's interior. They are carpeted with low, swarthy vegetation – including crape myrtle, which in summer adds splashes of colour to the landscape with its purple blooms – and pockmarked with boulders. You can also choose which way to head. On the left is the Rugged Trail, a rough track through the scrub and across bare rock that strikes out along the ridge, then angles

Hikers arriving at the junction of Po Toi's main trail and the Rugged Trail

Signpost to Old Mo's House, plus sign telling visitors to keep out

Peaceful pool

down to the temple. On the right is the concrete trail towards Po Toi's southern headland. This soon reaches Ngau Wu Teng, which is the highest point on Po Toi, 188m (617ft) above sea level. Here there is a pavilion with cracking views over the sea and islands to the south, beyond which the concrete trail abruptly tumbles off the ridge and onto the headland.

'While you are wandering on Po Toi Island,' advised a website from the Islands District Council, 'remember to open your heart and let your imagination fly. Otherwise, you will not be able to look at the rocks in another perspective and [will] miss the turtles, the monks, and even the unicorns and castles on [sic] the clouds.' This southern headland is just the place for looking at rocks with your imagination flying, as it boasts Turtle Rock, Monk Rock, Supine Monk and Palm Rock – and even if

the rocks look only like rocks, this is a fine place to visit.

A path along the spine of the headland leads to a squat automatic lighthouse, then turns down to the west. There is a trail from here to the tip of the headland. Here the granite has been stripped bare. It is cut with deep fissures, dotted with small pools – if you let fly with your imagination, it looks more like the surface of another planet than a corner of Hong Kong.

This vies with one of the Soko Islands for being the southernmost land in Hong Kong; it is also one of the territory's wildest and most dramatic headlands, with the sea forever churning and tugging at the cliffs below.

From the tip of the headland a trail winds along the coast, towards the cove. It passes the granite sculpted by the elements into Palm Rock – which really does look like a hand – skirts a tiny beach, then crosses a

Natural sculpture - Palm Rock indeed resembles a Buddha statue's hand

A drone's eye view of Po Toi's southernmost headland

Is your imagination flying? If yes, you'll see Turtle Rock here

small footbridge. There are steps down to a rock carving, but while this is of historic interest it is far from spectacular to look at.

The path runs through abandoned fields, where controversy flared in 2012 when a company built crude 'vaults' for storing urns. Villagers and environmentalists objected to the scheme and the columbarium plans were halted, while conservationists proposed designating

Would you call this Monk Rock?

much of Po Toi as country park. The trail then crosses the patio of a farmhouse that has become a simple restaurant – not a great place to eat, perhaps, but a boon on hot days when even carbonated drinks are like nectar of the gods, especially when they are fresh from the fridge. Past here the trail is close to the ferry pier.

It is possible to now set off to complete a figure-of-eight tour of Po Toi, by walking back up to the ridge and taking the Rugged Trail. If that seems excessive, there is a far easier way to the temple at the trail's end. Head through the ageing seaweed shop, and keep to the path through the village by the cove. There is a footbridge across a stream, with a tranquil pool on the right. Then there's a seafood restaurant, and buildings at the heart of the village. Beside them are big old banyan trees that, like other woodland patches, sometimes attract good numbers of migrant songbirds, including occasional strays that are rare for

Po Toi's Tin Hau temple, as if safeguarding the main village area

Hong Kong or even China.

There are tiny houses, and the path arrives at the temple perched on a headland at the mouth of the cove. As you would expect of a temple in a Hong Kong fishing community, this is dedicated to Tin Hau. There is not much to see inside, but the temple courtyard is a pleasant spot in which to linger, watching boats coming and going.

All being well, there is now time for a well-earned meal, before joining the crowds for the wander to the pier.

Getting there

• The kaito ferry is operated by Tsui Wah Ferry Service (www.traway.com.hk/渡輪服務/), and heads to Po Toi from a pier in Aberdeen on Tuesdays, Thursdays, Saturdays, Sundays and public holidays. It is also possible to catch this ferry when it leaves Blake Pier in Stanley on Sundays and public holidays.

Notes

• The Countryside Series map *Hong Kong Island & Neighbouring Islands* is useful.

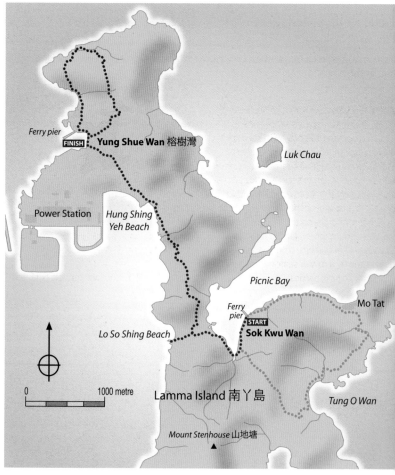

Ferry pier

FINISH **Yung Shue Wan** 榕樹灣

Luk Chau

Power Station

Hung Shing Yeh Beach

Picnic Bay

Mo Tat

Ferry pier

START **Sok Kwu Wan**

Lo So Shing Beach

Lamma Island 南丫島

Tung O Wan

0   1000 metre

Mount Stenhouse 山地塘

Sok Kwu Wan to Yung Shue Wan on Lamma Island

Lamma Island
Pier to pier

5km (3 miles) **

A simple route connects coastal villages, crossing green hillsides and passing beaches on Hong Kong's third largest island.

As the ferry nears Sok Kwu Wan, the east coast of Lamma appears almost unspoilt – hills run down to a coast with clusters of houses. However, as the ferry enters Picnic Bay for the final approach, a huge old quarry can be seen to scar the inlet's north side, although thanks to a rehabilitation project it is no longer the eyesore of yore.

The ferry berths on the inlet's unscathed southern shore. The village of Sok Kwu Wan, just 6km (4 miles) from Aberdeen, is dominated by a row of seafood restaurants that cater to junk parties.

Signposts for the Lamma Family Trail point left and right from the ferry pier. To the left lies Mo Tat village, on a loop that takes in old fields, a quiet coastline and the east flank of Mount Stenhouse, Lamma's highest peak.

For this outing turn right for a route leading to the island's other main ferry pier, at Yung Shue Wan. Pass a row of restaurants, then a small temple and trees with roots sprawling across boulders.

The path crosses a stream and turns north. Beside it there are tunnels cut into

View over Sok Kwu Wan, aka Picnic Bay

Yung Shue Wan - largest settlement on Hong Kong's third largest island

the foot of the hillside, reputedly during the Japanese occupation – a sign calls them Kamikaze Grottoes.

A Kamikaze Grotto, tunnel to nowhere

At a school and just before the Art Deco shelter of the Lo So Shing sitting out area, turn left through a break in the hills. The low, flat land is patterned with banana groves, fields and marshes; above the school and the houses on the opposite slopes there are woods and grassy hilltops.

Reaching a junction, there is a side trail to Lo So Shing Beach, on the west coast of Lamma. Set in a bay backed by low, wooded hills, the beach affords fine views to Cheung Chau and Lantau Islands. The views are tempered by the power station, which looms over the bay's northernmost headland.

The relatively remote Lo So Shing Beach

From a rocky promontory, southern Lamma still looks wild, with rugged Mount Stenhouse dropping steeply to the sea. The beach may be clean here; the water quality mostly receives a Grade One rating. All that is needed for swimming is Grade One weather.

Then back to the family trail and turn north again, through the village of Lo So Shing. The path climbs, leaves the woodland and reaches the crest of a slope above the former quarry. Minutes later, with the works hidden from view, the path rambles across west-facing slopes dotted with boulders that have made it only part way to the sea.

After a pavilion the path leads gently down to the beach at Hung Shing Yeh. This faces the power station, which seems immense and alien.

There are three-storey apartment blocks above the beach: lying 20 minutes away from the northern pier for ferries to Central, Hung Shing Yeh is expanding as weekenders and commuters move in.

Onwards and northwards the path leads through a landscape that is also changing as north Lamma becomes, increasingly, a Hong Kong suburb and retreat from high-price, high-pressure housing. Fields are disappearing and village boundaries are blurring as new housing is built to cash in on the trend.

Westerners are prominent among the new arrivals. 'Sale Come In' announced one of the hand-written signs at a small shop as I walked through one day. Among the goods on offer were flapjacks and lasa; none of the signs was in Chinese.

Yung Shue Wan is a huddle of houses and terraces beside its bay. The footpath

The beach at Hung Shing Yeh is near Lamma's main village and the power station

Temple at Sok Kwu Wan, dedicated to Tin Hau – goddess of the sea

that serves as the high street is lined with market stalls, shops, bars and restaurants. Inevitably, the restaurants offer an abundance of seafood, as well as, on some menus, Sunday roast beef.

The village ends by the ferry pier, where steps lead up between houses to a junction rejoining the family trail. A sign points the way to Po Wah Yuen and Pak Kok, Lamma's northernmost point. As the path levels out, the houses end and Lamma is quiet again. On the hillside above there may be Black Drongos perched on rocks or making acrobatic sallies after insects.

The path crests a ridge next to a rain shelter beside a picnic site. Around a corner to the east are rolling fields with villages named after Pak Kok. From close up the point looks uninteresting. So it's back to the ferry pier.

En route there is a path that leads beyond the rain shelter to a boulder-strewn hilltop. This is a good place to rest and enjoy the day's finest views of Lamma, with Mount Stenhouse as a backdrop to inlets, headlands and villages (only the tops of the power station's chimneys are in sight).

Then back to Yung Shue Wan, and the ferry to Central.

Getting there
• The Hong Kong and Kowloon Ferry (www. hkkf.com.hk) operates between Central and Sok Kwu Wan and Yung Shue Wan. Other licensed ferries operate between Aberdeen and Sok Kwu Wan.

Notes
• The Countryside Series map *Hong Kong Island & Neighbouring Islands* is useful.

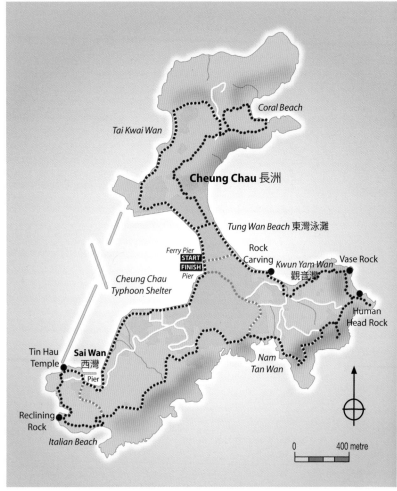

A Cheung Chau Explorer's Map

Cheung Chau
Isle of the Northern King

8.5km (5¼ miles) **

Lying off the south-east coast of Lantau, Cheung Chau looks tiny on the map. However, as in the case of Doctor Who's Tardis, this appearance is deceptive and there is much to explore, including coastal trails past naturally sculpted rocks.

Cheung Chau's main village area, and Lantau beyond

Densely packed housing near the typhoon shelter – and ferry pier

As you arrive at Cheung Chau the ferry passes fishing junks moored in the typhoon shelter; the island retains a thriving fishing community. If it is early on a weekday morning, you will have passed ferries packed with people bound for Central; Cheung Chau is also home to increasing numbers of commuters.

The island is formed by two lumps of granite linked by a low causeway running from north to south. The pier and much of the housing is on the causeway. The only car here is a small electric police car. Bicycles and pedal carts are available for hire, but – like early Daleks thwarted in their plans to conquer the universe – they are of little use when faced with the frequent steps. So the best way of getting around is by walking.

Nowadays the area near the pier may be throbbing with visitors. Do not despair, though – most do not go far. To explore, head left or right from the pier; if the beach is your aim, head for the opposite shore of the causeway.

Walking along the waterfront to the left takes you past rows of shops and restaurants, which give way to a football pitch. Turn right here and you arrive at Pak Tai Temple, where the island's chief god, Pak

Daurian Redstart, a winter visitor

Tai (the Northern King), gazes out to the sea.

Each spring the temple and the basketball court below it become the focus of the Bun Festival. Bamboo, plastic string and tin sheets are fashioned into a grand shed for operas and ceremonies by priests, a shelter for three gods and the towers that hold the steamed buns. Part homage to Pak Tai, who is credited with stemming two outbreaks of the plague, the festival is also a grand exorcism: after wandering ghosts have feasted on the buns, they are banished to the underworld.

A path leads uphill from beside the temple, passing under an archway noting

'Home for the aged'. Not everyone living beyond the archway is aged, though they might feel it after climbing the flight of steps.

The steps lead to a small, concrete-covered playground. From here, turn right and go uphill again. You soon leave the housing behind and reach grassy hills. Pass the service reservoir, and there is a track to a hilltop pavilion with views over Cheung Chau, and to Lamma and Hong Kong Island, and across to Lantau.

You could walk down flights of steps from here, onto a headland below, then to the secluded beach at Tung Wan Tsai. There is another path up from the north end of the beach, to a rough trail along the hillside, back towards the pavilion.

A wide track curves down the side of a valley with old farms set among trees and bamboo, and a housing estate in the lower reaches. It meets a coast road that is often busy with cycles and pedal carts. Turn left at the junction and you will soon pass an ice factory and return to 'town'.

Then it is back to the ferry pier. From the public pier beside the ferry pier, you can catch a sampan to the village of Sai Wan, near the south-west tip of the island. Or you can walk, turning right soon after the public pier, to follow the waterfront promenade.

Signposts at Sai Wan show the way over a headland to Cheung Po Tsai's Cave, which you can also reach via a small temple. Cheung Po Tsai was a 19th-century pirate who commanded hundreds of vessels and raided shipping along the south China coast. Despite local folklore stating that he cached his booty here, there is no real evidence to link him with the cave, which is little more than a cleft in the rock.

From above the cave a narrow flight of steps drops steeply between trees and boulders. The steps are the beginning of a path that runs south, then east, along the coast, to a narrow cove where you have to scramble over rocks (this part may be difficult or even impassable at high tide). The way then continues across a headland, passing a giant boulder that is suspended above the rocky shore, and reaches a cove with a beach, where a path leads up beside trees and an abandoned farmhouse.

Less interesting, but shorter and easier, is the path that runs through Sai Wan, southwards and away from the harbour at first, then turning eastwards and meeting the path from the beach.

Whichever route you take, continue eastwards along Peak Road, which winds gently uphill through a cemetery, then along the crest of southwestern Cheung Chau. Rural at first, the path soon passes housing, then returns to the main residential area – a sure sign you are nearing the ferry pier.

For more exploring take a right turn towards Nam Tan, a bay on the south coast with a Tin Hau temple. Above the tiny beach there is a path up through trees, and you can turn right along a coastal path. This path angles around a headland, and there is a junction where you can keep right, above a steep slope dropping to the sea. After angling uphill a little, turn right by a walled housing compound.

The path arrives by another headland. Here there is a chance for a side trip along an overgrown path to an abandoned building that was perhaps grand in decades gone by – maybe it was a holiday place for missionaries working in China – but is now ruined, with a banyan tree growing into a wall. A small

statue of the Virgin Mary long resided on a plinth amid the rampant vegetation, but it has recently been spirited away.

Onwards the trail is again above the sea. There is a junction by a cluster of buildings, with a path leading down an east-facing hillside and arriving at the Mini Great Wall. As you will notice, this is not a wall but a path made of marble-like blocks winding around headlands, a very, very little like the Great Wall of China crossing mountains. Below here a large tor has been sculpted by weather so that it now perches on a narrow support – imaginative people have called it Human Head Rock.

Crested Goshawks prey on woodland birds

Nam Tan, on the south coast, is among the scenic spots awaiting anyone willing to explore beyond the main village

Vase Rock, and night lights of Hong Kong and Lamma islands

There is a right turn to a viewpoint perched on top of a low cliff above the steep south-east coast of Cheung Chau. You need even more imagination to make out nearby Zombie Rock. Then it is back to the human head and northwards along the path, with signs indicating more naturally sculpted outcrops, including Elephant Rock.

There are steps down to Flower Vase Rock, which may not look vase-like from this angle but is scenic, with views eastwards towards Lamma and Hong Kong Island. Onwards and northwards you soon leave the Mini Great Wall, arrive at a lookout pavilion, then drop down to Kwun Yam Wan.

If you ignore the right turn to Nam Tam and keep to Peak Road, soon there is the Kwan Kung Pavilion on the right. This is a temple to Kwan Kung, originally a general, who has become a god for both the triads (aka black societies) and the police. In early spring flowering trees in the tiny garden here can attract crowds of photographers.

Then there is a downhill stretch. Part way down, at the base of a large tree, is a marker for an old residential boundary that was aimed at keeping the southern part of Cheung Chau a classy area (much as on Hong Kong Island's Peak, this may have meant excluding Chinese). Nowadays, of course, the whole island is classy, and the ferry journey helps to deter riffraff from taking up residence.

Peak Road ends at a junction soon after

Getting there
- New World First Ferry (www.nwff.com.hk) has ferries between Central and Cheung Chau. There is also a ferry linking Cheung Chau with Lantau and Peng Chau a few times a day.

Notes
- The Countryside Series map *Lantau Island & Neighbouring Islands* is useful.

the Royal Hong Kong Jockey Club. Should you head left you could wander Cheung Chau's winding, narrow streets. You might also get lost.

Maybe it is better, then, to turn right into Tai San Back Street, and keep on until you reach the sacred banyan, credited with maintaining the island's prosperity Some islanders have reportedly adopted it as godfather to their children, hoping that they will grow up smart and strong.

Turn right at the tree and you will come to Tung Wan Beach. Turn right again and below Cheung Chau's largest building, the Warwick Hotel, you will find the ancient rock carving.

After gazing in awe at the carving, walk on a little, to arrive at Kwun Yam Wan, with a beach smaller than at Tung Wan though still popular with swimmers. There are a couple of small bars here; perhaps take a

seat at the Windsurfing Centre and relax after the exploring. In the bay there may be windsurfers doing their thing, or trying to, anyway – in summer there is often little wind (zealots await near-misses by typhoons); the best season is autumn, with its gusty cold fronts.

If it is summer the beaches may be crowded; they have showers and changing facilities, which are also handy after a hot day's exploring.

The sun drops behind Lantau and it is time for dinner. Cheung Chau boasts an abundance of seafood restaurants: try along along the waterfront towards Pak Tai Temple. As the evening wears on, bars along the waterfront and the road with the sacred tree draw a mix of regulars and newcomers. If you are a bit of a night owl you could sample two or three bars, then catch a late ferry to Central.

Former grandeur – a ruined house being reclaimed by nature

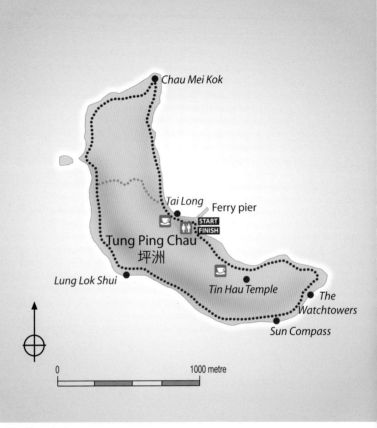

Tung Ping Chau circuit

Tung Ping Chau

Flat but fascinating

6km (4 miles) *

Tung Ping Chau is a far-flung island with mostly abandoned villages, resurgent woodland, beaches and scenic rock formations.

Walking off the pier during my early visits to Ping Chau ('Flat Island'), as it was then simply known, I saw a prominent sign saying: 'Passengers are advised not to visit the outlying islands unless they have checked in advance that a reliable means of return transport is available.' The sign has gone, yet the advice remains sound, as Hong Kong's islands do not come any more outlying than this.

By the time the ferry heading there rounds the north coast of the island, the hills of Sai Kung and Plover Cove Country Park are little more than low shapes in the haze, and mainland China dominates the view. The green, hilly peninsula that bounds eastern Mirs Bay is so close that, through binoculars, resorts, fishing villages, roads and people walking on beaches can be clearly seen.

Yet while nearby Guangdong flourishes, this far-flung, improbable outpost of Hong Kong seems set on its own, contrary course. In the days when Shenzhen was barely a twinkle in the Chinese government's eyes and the peninsula was surely little inhabited, Ping Chau's population was reportedly more than 1,000.

Today, with most houses abandoned and crumbling, the island is home to just two old men, and only at weekends do the remaining villages come alive. Campers and day-trippers arrive on the ferry. There are also island people who might live in new

Corals grow in the relatively clear waters off eastern Tung Ping Chau

Tung Ping Chau at sunset, from a homeward-bound ferry

towns, but can still call Tung Ping Chau home (the 'Tung' – East – helps distinguish it from Peng Chau, western Hong Kong). Carrying provisions, they head for their houses on Saturdays and some holidays, there to meet friends, set up stalls selling soft drinks and cooked food, and stay overnight.

At Tai Tong village a little north of the pier, I used to book a room and leave my belongings in it before exploring. However, the government has since banned villagers from operating mini guest houses. Even the simple restaurants faced issues, though they reopened. At one of these, some years ago, I talked to a Ping Chau devotee who had been visiting the island for more than 20 years. In the early 1970s, he told me, robberies by people from China were so frequent that everyone left; only two old men had returned to live on the island. I asked about smuggling, which was reputedly rife. After a pause, he said only, 'That does not happen now.'

From Tai Tong there is a footpath heading inland. It leads to a cluster of derelict houses set in a wood where the only sounds are of bamboo swaying and scraping in the wind. Some buildings have collapsed, others are tumbledown, but there are a few you can walk into through gaping doorways, and perhaps find the remnants of stone stoves along with utensils like clay jars.

During spring and autumn this is sometimes a good place for birdwatching, perhaps with sightings of insect-eating songbirds such as warblers and flycatchers. Tung Ping Chau can attract fair densities of migrants, though fewer than Po Toi, which is far more popular with birdwatchers.

The path ends at a water tank, so discovering more of the island requires backtracking. There is a left turn, with a chance to head up a low hill, towards the police station – this is still used by the Marine Police, partly as a base to help combat modern-day smuggling across Mirs Bay. Turning left again, there is a former army training camp. This is now Hong Kong's only radiation shelter – Tung Ping Chau is just 12km (7½ miles) from the Daya Bay Nuclear Power Station. A rough track skirts around the camp, and drops down to the island's west coast. On my visits, however, I sometimes turn back to Tai Tong and halt for lunch.

The beach is close by. There are stretches of fine white sand, and outcroppings of the mudstone that makes up the island and is found nowhere else in Hong Kong. Unlike the volcanic material forming most of Hong Kong, this is sedimentary rock. Formed around 65 million years ago from silt that accumulated in a basin that is present-day Mirs Bay, it is the youngest rock in Hong Kong.

The sea is a classic tropical blue; coral chunks scattered along the tideline hint at the attractions of snorkelling here. There are colourful fish, sea urchins, and corals like vertical plates and exotic castles in the shallow waters, which are protected in one of Hong Kong's four marine parks.

At the north end of the island the path leaves the beach, climbs and runs above a low cliff.

Tung Ping Chau is in the shape of a crescent, roughly 2km (1¼ miles) long and never more than 700m (2,300ft) wide. Along its inner, eastern arc, the layers of the mudstone slope gently into the sea, but

Trail above the west coast

elsewhere the rock is sliced away, forming the cliffs.

The path curves and follows the clifftop southwards. The island's rolling landscape, no longer farmed, is carpeted with long grasses and shrubs, with woods hiding the old villages. The main feature along the west coast is a rock formation known as Lung Lok

Layers of mudstone, youngest rock in Hong Kong, east Tung Ping Chau

Lung Lok Shui: Dragon Descending to the Sea

The Ping Chau Watchtowers

Shui: Dragon Descending to the Sea. It is a mini escarpment – not much taller than a person – dipping beneath the waves, and is capped by a serrated band of chert, formed of microcrystalline quartz that is more resistant to erosion than the mudstone.

At the southern end of the island the path reaches the highest point, a modest 48m (160ft) above sea level. There is a 'sun compass' with arrows pointing in the directions of sunset and sunrise at different times of the year.

Then, down to a place where the cliffs have all but eroded away, leaving two stubborn, tor-like masses: the Ping Chau Watchtowers. Below them the sea meets rock that resists in rows, or is torn away in slabs to leave erratic, zigzag steps and suddenly deep rock pools. This is a popular area for visitors and for landscape photography.

From here it is only a short walk back to the pier. The route follows the rocky, pebble-strewn shoreline and soon arrives at a hamlet. Here there are more simple shops – it's a good place, perhaps, to halt for a chilled drink before catching the ferry.

Getting there
- Tsui Wah Ferry Service (www.traway.com.hk/渡輪服務/) operates ferries to the island from Ma Liu Shui (15 minutes' walk from the University East Rail station). They depart at 9 p.m. on Saturdays, Sundays and public holidays; return ferries are at 5.15 p.m. It is advisable to arrive early at Ma Liu Shui, as ferry seats are limited and the island outing has become extremely popular.

Notes
- Food and drinks are available on the island. It is wise to have repellent against mosquitoes, and ants may abound. The latter nip rather than sting, but still encourage a brisk walk where they occur.
- There are map boards near the ferry pier and the sun compass. Tung Ping Chau is included in the Countryside Series map *North-East & Central New Territories*.

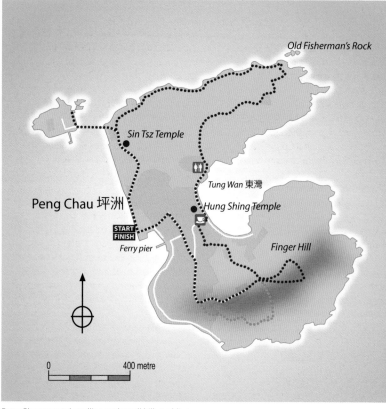

Old Fisherman's Rock

Sin Tsz Temple

Tung Wan 東灣

Peng Chau 坪洲

Hung Shing Temple

START
FINISH

Ferry pier

Finger Hill

0   400 metre

Peng Chau coastal strolling and small hill rambling

Peng Chau
In search of a quiet life

5.5km (3½ miles) *

Though Peng Chau has similarities to Cheung Chau, it is smaller and quieter – with a more rural, perhaps more introverted character. Rather like Cheung Chau, the main village is in the centre of the island, and there are hilly areas with trails to the west and east.

Ferries arrive on the island's west coast. From the pier there is a broad avenue lined with impressive banyan trees, leading past a humungous Regional Council Complex to a Tin Hau Temple, which is on the narrow main street.

Rather than heading straight for the village centre, you might first turn left, towards north Peng Chau. You pass housing blocks along the waterfront; some are recently built, as if developers are aiming to establish a kind of upmarket suburb. Perhaps lost among the new construction are the ruins of old buildings, which were once part of the largest match factory in Southeast Asia.

Shrine to the Seventh Sister

The narrow road soon arrives at a cluster of three tiny temples. The most obvious of them is the shrine to the Seventh Sister, which is wonderfully colourful – the Seventh Sister is associated with the colours of the rainbow. The other temples are dedicated to the Monkey King and the Buddhist Guan Yin.

A little past the temples there is a bridge to an islet. Across this you can walk onto a narrow shingle beach. Marine biologists have identified 35 coral species in the waters here: a remarkable tally for western Hong Kong, which is influenced by the Pearl River and away from the more oceanic eastern waters. In the past these corals, plus seashells, formed the basis of a substantial lime industry on Peng Chau.

There is little more to the islet, so head back to the shore of Peng Chau and join the Peng Yu Path. After a short flight of steps up, it dips to a small bay with a short, sandy beach. Here the coast of Peng Chau seems wild and almost remote, with only trees and shrubs clothing the hillside – but Hong Kong Disneyland is in view, only a short way across the sea.

There is rocky shoreline, and soon another beach. Like the first beach it is perhaps not too good for swimming – especially as there is no lifeguard service – but it can be fun for picnicking, paddling and checking out nearby rock pools. The path climbs a little, and there is a shelter, then more steps leading down to the end of the trail by the high tideline.

Boulevard to Lung Mo Temple

There must have been a headland here before, but it has been eroded away, leaving only remnants. Across the top of a beach there is a rocky knoll capped by a tor, an isolated tower of granite resisting the elements – Old Fisherman's Rock. A little scrambling around the knoll leads to another tor, on a low rocky platform that waves surge across.

From the shelter steps lead up the hillside. There is a junction, and after a right turn there are trees and bamboo thickets affording shade that is welcome on a hot day. At another junction there is a left turn, and the trail leads past one of Peng Chau's most distinctive landmarks, a radio station's transmission tower at the crest of the headland.

From here a path winds down into a small valley, passing small orchards with lychee, banana, guava and jackfruit trees. The farmhouses are mostly shanty style, with some looking run down. There are vegetable fields, too, and at least one organic farm, before the path arrives at the deep inlet known as Tung Wan – east bay, which is set between the peninsulas of north and south Peng Chau.

The main village is at the head of the

bay. Almost in the centre of the buildings fringing the bay is a red-brick temple dedicated to Lung Mo, the Dragon Mother. Beside this an alley leads to Wing On Street, the Street of Eternal Peace, and the temple dedicated to Tin Hau, the goddess of the sea. A stone tablet beside this dates from the Qing dynasty, and it tells of a decree that when soldiers were chasing pirates, they were not permitted to commandeer islanders' fishing boats.

Walk south along the main street and it almost tunnels between the buildings. Shops and small restaurants are packed tightly together, and face each other across a thoroughfare barely wider than a city footpath. Even narrower alleyways lead

Getting there
• Hong Kong and Kowloon Ferry Holdings (www.hkkf.com.hk) operate ferries between Central and Peng Chau.

Notes
•The Countryside Series map *Lantau Island & Neighbouring Islands* is useful, though not essential.

Fields and small farmhouses

off to left and right, disappearing into the tightly packed jumble of houses.

The main street ends near the foot of a hill. From here there are various paths, including at least one signposted towards Finger Hill, which at 95m (312ft) is the highest point on the island. A flight of steps leads up from the western flank of the hill, and reaches a vantage with panoramic views over much of Peng Chau, nearby Lantau and Kau Sai Chau, and east to Hong Kong Island.

The headland with Old Fisherman's Rock, west Peng Chau

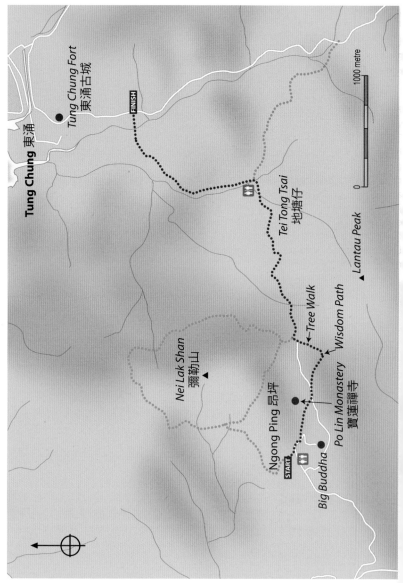

Ngong Ping and down to Tung Chung

Po Lin to Tung Chung

Once there were pilgrims   9km (5½ miles) to 11.5km (7 miles) **

Enjoy trails amid fabulous upland scenery, before heading down a hillside towards Lantau's north coast.

For decades the way to Po Lin Monastery was by the Pilgrim's Path. Beginning at Tai O on the west coast of Lantau, this led halfway up Lantau Peak, to the Ngong Ping plateau. Especially because Lantau was remote and sparsely populated, it was not a route to encourage casual visitors. This is just as well, perhaps, for in the monastery's early years casual visitors were unlikely to have been welcome. Po Lin – or Precious Lotus – was established in 1905 by three reclusive monks who chose the site for

their meditations. For shelter, they built stone huts.

How different things are today. Po Lin is now one of the largest and most visited monasteries in Hong Kong. It even has its own bus routes: the way now begins not at Tai O, but on Lantau's opposite, east shore, at the Mui Wo (Silvermine Bay) ferry pier; or on the north shore, at Tung Chung.

Board the bus from Mui Wo and you may find that it soon fills with day-trippers before departing. Like a roller coaster being

The Big Buddha; and clouds swirling about Lantau Peak

Once a place for pilgrims, Ngong Ping is now a hotspot for tourists, with the Big Buddha a key draw

cranked up the initial slope, the bus climbs out of Mui Wo, passing through woodland and by cattle loitering on the verge. Then the bus starts careening along Lantau's southern coast – passing through Pui O, Cheung Sha, Tong Fuk and Shui Hau. After Shek Pik the driver tilts at the hill, then turns onto the winding highway that brings Po Lin its visitors, and dollars.

The highway and journey end at an expanse of concrete rivalling the Mui Wo terminus. Beside this, stalls sell drinks, snacks and souvenirs. Nearby is the monastery, modern and colourful. Prominent among the decor – its image patterns the floor of the main hall – is the lotus flower, an important emblem of Buddhist faith. If such beauty can grow from mud and stagnant water, reason Buddhists, anyone can attain enlightenment.

As if to remind visitors of enlightenment – and of the possible shortcut to a better afterlife through making worthy donations – the big bronze Buddha sits on a nearby hilltop, gazing across the bus stop to Po Lin. A flight of steps leads to the base of the statue (at 26.4m/866ft the largest seated, outdoor bronze statue of Buddha in the world), from where there are great views of the monastery and surrounding area.

A sign by the bus terminus points to the Tea Gardens. The path leads through a mix of woodland and tea plantations. It passes an overgrown paddock, where horse rides were once offered. Then there is a cluster of buildings, including the sadly abandoned Tea Gardens Restaurant. Close by is a tiny remnant of the former tea plantation that was established in 1947, albeit with too hot a climate for the Lotus Brand tea to be of premium quality.

The trees beside the path give out, and there is a wooden archway with the legend 'Lantau Trail'. Immediately beyond it rises

the sharp cone of Lantau Peak. On the right is the Wisdom Path, a short, looped path beside skeletons of tropical trees that were cut down and brought here, with Buddhist inscriptions carved on them. Above these is a low hill that affords impressive views over Ngong Ping, including the Buddha, and across Shek Pik Reservoir to the Soko Islands.

Turn left just before the archway and there is a rough trail that doubles as a tree walk. It ends at a concrete path, and there is a choice of routes. Ngong Ping is nearby to the left.

Opposite, there is a short path up to the Nei Lak Shan Country Trail, a 5km (3-mile) circuit of Nei Lak Shan that almost follows contours. You can walk halfway – taking the southern route with fine views overlooking the Big Buddha, or going along the north slope looking out across the airport – then drop down to the Ngong Ping Village (more a wannabe tourist trap than a village). Or perhaps follow the entire circuit and return to this junction.

There is also a path northwards, towards Tung Chung. It angles down the north slopes of Lantau Peak. Beside a bend in the trail a pavilion offers a chance to rest and enjoy the view. There are hills on three sides, while the slopes below give way to a broad valley with the fields and villages of Tung Chung. Beyond Tung Chung, across a bay, lie the airport and a lonesome little hill, which is

The secluded Po Lam Monastery

Along the Nei Lak Shan Country Trail

all that remains of Chek Lap Kok, an island sacrificed on the altar of economic progress.

Further down is Tei Tong Tsai. It is one of Lantau's five main Buddhist sites, and unlike Po Lin it remains peaceful. It is almost eerily peaceful, perhaps, with some buildings looking abandoned. At Po Lam Monastery it seems that the nuns favour seclusion. The site can be reached only by footpaths set among a stand of large trees and bamboo, and it is clearly poorer than Po Lin, which is boisterous by comparison.

There is a junction, with another country trail to the right, and a path to Tung Chung on the left. The Tung Chung path tumbles down alongside a stream that has carved a shallow ravine. Then the slope eases, and the path runs above the ravine before turning right and down again.

Near the foot of the slope the path meets a narrow road, and passes the unimposing Lo Hon Monastery and a smattering of houses. In the past I walked paths through new fields towards the former fishing hamlet of Ma Wan Chung, but now new housing covers much of the lowland here, and work is underway on further construction projects. It is thus best to end the walk around here and perhaps head for home.

Alternatively head to Tung Chung Fort, which is by the road to the town centre, just under a kilometre to the north. The fort dates from early last century and is one of several forts built in Hong Kong to help guard against pirates and to control foreign trading ships. Judging by its location and Chinese records, it was more an administrative centre than a proper fort. Today thick walls – one of them topped with cannons – surround buildings housing a school, the rural committee and a visitor centre.

Once you have seen the fort you can cross the road and turn left, past Yat Tung Estate, to the edge of Tung Chung Bay. Soon you come to an old banyan tree complete with a shrine. Further on, by the shoreline, is Hau Wong Temple. Perhaps built in 1765, this honours a general who strived to protect the last emperor of the Song dynasty from pursuing Mongol forces.

A footbridge crosses Tung Chung Stream, where you might find kingfishers or herons. Just beyond it, unless it is low tide, there is a simple path along the the stream channel out into the bay. On warm days the tidal mudflats here come alive with mudskippers – small, air breathing fish – and fiddler crabs waving their outsize claws. Mangrove trees are adapted to life in the tidal zone, and there are small beds of eelgrass, which is one of only a few flowering plants at home in the sea.

Po Lin Monastery and Lantau Peak

Nei Lak Shan Country Trail

Getting there

- New World First Ferry (www.nwff.com.hk) has ferries linking Central with Mui Wo (Silvermine Bay). Buses to Po Lin ('Ngong Ping') depart from the Mui Wo ferry pier. Or you can travel by MTR or bus to Tung Chung, and catch a bus to Ngong Ping from there.
- Ngong Ping 360 cable car offers another way of travelling to Ngong Ping, from Tung Chung near the airport. Food and drinks are available at Po Lin; the monastery's vegetarian restaurant is popular though rather fast-food style.
- By Lo Hon Monastery, at the foot of the slope, there is a stop for minibus 34, which serves the Tung Chung area, including the town centre. However, it is infrequent, so it may be better to walk right to Tung Chung Road and catch a bus to Mui Wo, or to Tung Chung new town (perhaps alighting by the fort).

Notes

- The Countryside Series map *Lantau Island & Neighbouring Islands* is useful.

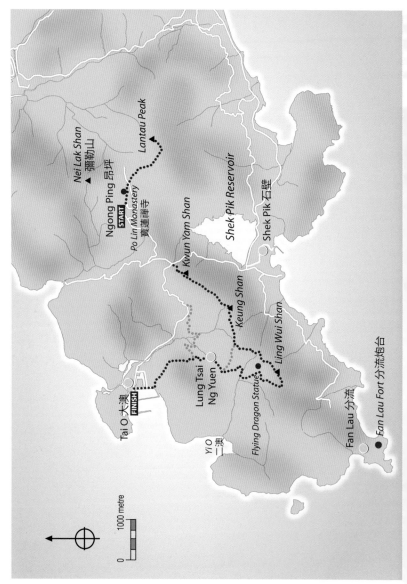

Lantau Peak, and a south-west Lantau hike

Nei Lak Shan 彌勒山

Lantau Peak

Ngong Ping 昂坪
START
Po Lin Monastery 寶蓮禪寺

Shek Pik Reservoir

Shek Pik 石壁

Kwun Yam Shan

Keung Shan

Ling Wui Shan

Lung Tsai Ng Yuen

Tai O 大澳
FINISH

Flying Dragon Statue

Yi O 二澳

Fan Lau 分流

Fan Lau Fort 分流炮台

0   1000 metre

Lantau Peak and South-west Lantau

Rising sun, flying dragon   4km + 8.5km (2½ miles + 5¼ miles)*****

Start the day with a pre-dawn climb before hiking Lantau's south-west hills, or perhaps head up Lantau Peak one day and save those lower hills for another time.

Path to Lantau Peak, in twilight

Scintillating summer day view from south-west Lantau

If you walk east from Ngong Ping's woodland before daybreak, Lantau Peak looms ahead: a black, massive cone against the night sky. High up the slopes there may be scattered points of light, as torches light the way of climbers in the darkness. As you follow them, torchlight soon picks out the first of many steps – I have read that there are 1,400 in all.

After climbing a few hundred of the steps, it may seem a good time to rest and look down at the receding lights of Po Lin Monastery and other buildings at Ngong Ping. Continue up, up, left and up, and the path turns to follow the spine of an exposed ridge, then a gentler stretch and final climb to Hong Kong's second highest summit.

There may already be a small crowd gathered to wait for the sunrise. A chill wind was blowing as I arrived before dawn one day. 'Ho tung (very cold),' I heard people saying as they huddled beneath blankets and sleeping bags, and sheltered behind rocks. I found a place away from the worst of the wind, lay back and looked at the night

Azalea at Lung Tsai Ng Yuen

sky. The stars were the brightest I had seen in Hong Kong. A shooting star flashed past and vanished as a tiny meteorite sizzled into nothingness.

With the sun still far away to the east, this high, remote hilltop seemed a fine place to reflect on life's important questions. Why am I here? Where am I going? Why am I not sound asleep in a nice warm bed?

The morning when I arrived before dawn the sunrise disappointed, and the sun

West slopes of Lantau Peak

was already glaringly bright as it emerged from behind low clouds. As on any fine day, however, the views were fabulous, including the South China Sea below to the south, and Sunset Peak nearby to the east.

Although it is downhill from here, the uneven, rocky steps can make the return to Ngong Ping slow going. Then there is a chance to explore more of Lantau – maybe heading for the lower, south-western hills.

Winding down the narrow road from Ngong Ping in the morning, the bus passes other buses that are bound for Po Lin and bursting with people. The monastery soon resonates with crowds.

At the junction with the Silvermine Bay to Tai O road, leave the bus, walk to the left, then start up stage five of the Lantau Trail. There are flights of steps, but if you have climbed 1,400 steps in pitch darkness they present no challenge.

After reaching a high point the trail follows a switchback of grassy hilltops as it aims for Ling Wui Shan, at 490m

Getting there

• New World First Ferry (www.nwff.com.hk) operates services between Central and Mui Wo (Silvermine Bay). Buses depart Mui Wo and Tung Chung for Ngong Ping; there are buses to Mui Wo and Tung Chung from Tai O, with stops along Tai O Road.

Notes

• At Ngong Ping, accommodation is available at the Hong Kong YHA's S. G. Davis Ngong Ping Youth Hostel, email info@yha.org.hk.
• If you hike up Lantau Peak for the sunrise, take a torch and be prepared for the cooler air on the summit.
• The Countryside Series map *Lantau Island & Neighbouring Islands* is useful.

(1,600ft) the highest point in south-west Lantau. This is a majestic vantage, with Macau to the west, Hong Kong Island to the east just visible on a clear day and Lantau Peak dominating the interior of the island. Once there, the trail drops down and turns right.

Lantau Peak is also called Fung Wong Shan - Phoenix Mountain

The lovely Lung Tsai Ng Yuen, surely Hong Kong's prime folly

Soon, on the right, there is the Flying Dragon. A stone and plaster statue, the dragon is a long, spindly beast, balancing on rocks above the Tsz Hing Monastery. Garishly painted and with its jaws open in a wild roar, it makes a bizarre addition to the landscape.

Past the monastery there is an expansive, rolling landscape. The trail crosses a stream, leads up a small valley, then turns away to the right and reaches another Lantau folly, Lung Tsai Ng Yuen.

An ornamental garden in classical Chinese style, Ng Yuen was built by the late Mr Woo Quen-sung. It was formerly open to the public and you could tour the garden, walking along corridors and grassy paths between summer houses and shrubberies.

With some buildings in disrepair

and a zigzag bridge across a carp pond deteriorating and dangerous, Ng Yuen was recently closed. There has since been some renovation work by the owners, but you need to be lucky to find the gate open, and for visitors to be allowed to wander the grounds. It is still an interesting place to look at, though, and best seen from the small dam the trail passes.

Stage five of the trail ends beside the garden, and stage six begins. This follows a concrete path, which is gentle at first, then drops steeply down to the coast. For a more pleasant route to the main road – and bus stops – turn right down a concrete path shortly after Ng Yuen, and right again at a catchwater road that hugs contours and will provide fine views, before reaching Tai O Road.

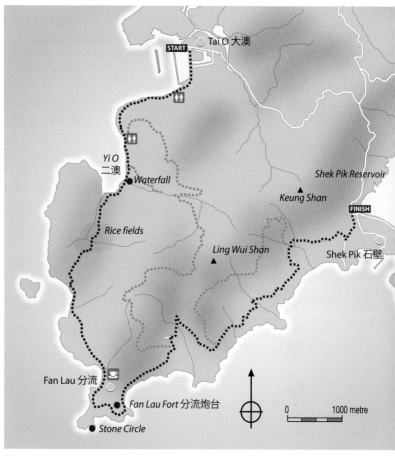

START

Tai O 大澳

Yi O
二澳

Waterfall

Rice fields

Shek Pik Reservoir

Keung Shan

FINISH

Ling Wui Shan

Shek Pik 石壁

Fan Lau 分流

Fan Lau Fort 分流炮台

Stone Circle

0   1000 metre

Coastal hike at south-west Lantau Island

Fan Lau
Historical relics and soft drinks

15km (9½ miles) ****

When walking coastal paths in south-west Lantau, you can admire fine scenery, halt at a waterfall plunge pool, and check out old villages and resurgent rice farming, and an old fort overlooking the South China Sea.

The trail south from beside Yi O rice fields

Fan Lau, the division of flows, is a near-forgotten outpost of Hong Kong, on the south-west peninsula of Lantau Island, once known mainly for a rumpus over abandoned plans for a power station, and the site of an old fort. With the nearest road perhaps three hours' walk away, it is a remote place, but makes a fine destination for a rewarding day out.

There are a few possible routes to Fan Lau, but the best is probably a mostly coastal walk, starting at Tai O. This initially passes an artificial lagoon with mangroves, joins the Lantau Trail and runs through villages, then climbs a little to become a woodland path.

The path starts to descend and there is a steep trail up to the left. This trail was built to bypass a nearby village, Yi O, where former residents once declared their area off limits to hikers. Happily the situation has since changed, and while the uphill path leads to a scenic hillside route, you can

Resurgent rice farming at Yi O

continue along the easier way, through Yi O. There is an inlet, where the path skirts a shoreline. After a bridge over a stream, you can take a diversion left through trees to a picturesque waterfall and plunge pool.

Further south the path turns inland and passes Yi O's cluster of derelict houses. Though the village is abandoned, a project to restart farming began in 2012. This centres on growing rice in paddyfields that are perhaps five minutes' walk beyond the old houses.

Walk between the paddyfields and up towards the base of farm operations – in the remnants of an older Yi O village – and there is a junction with the slender trail towards Fan Lau, heading into woodland. This follows an ancient pathway with boulders for steps, which leads up to a gap between the main Lantau hills and a hill that dominates a stubby peninsula.

There is a low, rocky wall at the highest

Yi O at low tide, looking south

Abandoned Fan Lau Fort; ferry bound for Macau

point between the hills – in times past, it probably marked the southernmost boundary of Yi O's territory. Then the path runs gently downhill. It drops down a short, steep flight of rough-hewn steps, and the route is by the coast again, close to a beach. It is a pleasant beach to stroll on, though the tideline may be strewn with plastic waste carried down the Pearl River and testifying to our throwaway society.

Soon there is another beach, as the path arrives at Fan Lau. Like Yi O village, this has clearly seen better days; several old houses are abandoned or in ruins. There are still some diehard individuals living here, and a couple of places sell drinks and simple fare. It is only about 500m (1,640ft) across the peninsula to another, more attractive beach.

Stroll towards the right along this beach, and at the southern end there is a path up towards the fort, which is on a hilltop near the tip of the peninsula. Though the fort was once divided into rooms, nowadays there is little left but thick stone walls enclosing empty space that is roughly the size of a tennis court.

An information board says that Fan Lau Fort was built in 1729, and overlooks a strategically important sea passage through the mouth of the Pearl River. It was manned until perhaps 1900, after which it fell into disrepair. There has been renovation work, in 1985 and again in 1990/91, and though brick paving was laid down, long grass has since regrown within the fort.

Through an entranceway there is a flight of steps to the top of the southernmost wall, which overlooks coastal waters travelled by ferries between Hong Kong and Macau.

Head south-west from the fort and you will see a rough path down towards a stone circle. No one knows when or why this circle

View north from a drone over Fan Lau

– which is really an oval – was built. Perhaps it is from Neolithic or Bronze Age times, a distant cousin of Europe's great ancient circles. However, unlike Stonehenge, say, there is no drama about this circle; the low ring of stones is curious but uninspiring, and protected by a tall mesh fence.

Below, the water lapping on the east-facing coast may look clearer than to the west of Fan Lau, which lies between the silty Pearl River outflow and the South China Sea.

Soon it is time to decide how to leave Fan Lau. One obvious route heads east along the Lantau Trail to Shek Pik. Mostly, however, this is just along a narrow road beside a catchwater, and makes for a dull trudge for what can seem kilometre after kilometre.

You can avoid most of this catchwater road by taking a turn up to the Keung Shan Country Trail, which starts a little east of the junction between stages seven and eight of

Fan Lau's unprepossessing yet mysterious stone circle

the Lantau Trail. This leads uphill, then almost follows contours to the east and north, finishing at a road junction below Ngong Ping. There are several stream crossings that require a little care, and which you should not attempt if the streams are in spate.

Other possibilities lead through the hills, or simply head back to Tai O via Yi O.

Getting there
- New World First Ferry (www.nwff.com.hk) operates regular ferries between Central and Mui Wo (Silvermine Bay). Buses to Tai O run from the Mui Wo ferry pier; they typically coincide with the arrival of the ferries from Central. Or you could take a bus or the MTR to Tung Chung, then a bus to Tai O.

Getting back
- Buses back to Mui Wo or Tung Chung can be caught near the end of the trail at Shek Pik.

Notes
- At Ngong Ping, accommodation is available at the Hong Kong YHA's S. G. Davis Ngong Ping Youth Hostel, email info@yha.org.hk.
- If you hike up Lantau Peak for the sunrise, take a torch and be prepared for the cooler air on the summit.
- The Countryside Series map *Lantau Island & Neighbouring Islands* is useful.

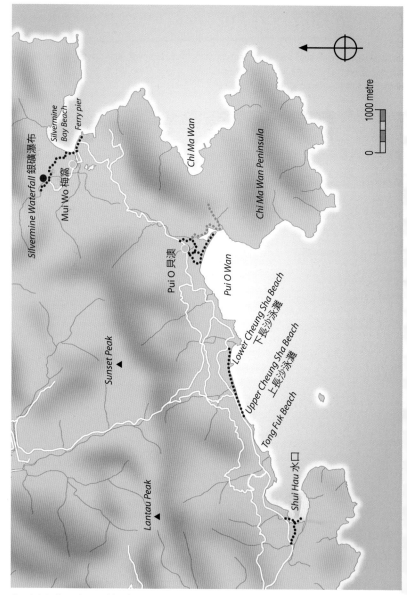

Silvermine Waterfall 銀鑛瀑布

Silvermine Bay Beach

Ferry pier

Mui Wo 梅窩

Chi Ma Wan

Chi Ma Wan Peninsula

Pui O 貝澳

Pui O Wan

Sunset Peak ▲

Lower Cheung Sha Beach 下長沙泳灘

Upper Cheung Sha Beach 上長沙泳灘

Tong Fuk Beach

Lantau Peak ▲

Shui Hau 水口

1000 metre

0

Coastal strolls on Lantau Island

Cheung Sha and Pui O
Beaches and buffaloes

6km (3¾ miles) *

On some days a simple stroll may seem more appealing than a hilly hike – and Cheung Sha's beach may be just the place to head for, perhaps along with one or more of the wonderful coastal areas of Hong Kong's largest and most beautiful island, Lantau.

Water Buffalo taking an evening stroll on Pui O Beach

Set on the still little-developed south coast of Lantau Island, Cheung Sha – 'Long Sands' – has the most extensive beach in Hong Kong. It is in two parts, separated by a mini headland, and makes for excellent strolling – and, of course, you can swim here.

Perhaps start at the western end, Upper Cheung Sha, where there is a building with showers above a gazetted beach that can be a top option for swimming. Behind, other than the building there is litttle but trees, the roads and the green slopes of Lantau's hills. In front is the South China Sea, dotted with small islets.

Walk east and – the road being further inland – the beach seems relatively wild, with expansive vistas of hills, sand, sea and sky. Often there are few people here: perhaps fishermen, sun-worshippers, glamour photographers with models, and picnicking families. There is a small water-sports centre, and outdoor enthusiasts might be bodyboarding or even arrive by paragliders after leaping from slopes far above.

Across the headland is the eastern beach, at Lower Cheung Sha. Here, too, there is a gazetted beach, plus restaurants in the small village above the tideline.

Eastwards lies another fine beach – at Pui O, along with a scruffy village, splendid scenery and former paddyfields roamed by feral water buffaloes.

Walk the narrow road from beside Pui O Public School, and you will soon find the old paddyfields to the left and right. You should see buffaloes here, too, perhaps grazing close by or plodding across the road. Though they look huge and fearsome, they are well used to people, and are chiefly focused on munching grass and wallowing in muddy pools. Late on hot days in particular, some may trundle to the beach and bathe in the sea. Watch for birds, too: egrets and herons are invariably present, with Cattle Egrets following buffaloes in case they startle tasty insects from hiding places.

The beach of dark, fine silt is good for swimming; it slopes gently, so the waters are shallow even some distance from the shore. It also affords top views, with nearby hills plunging to the south coast of Lantau. Turn right on arriving at the beach and you will come to a patch of low scrub and flowers, which in late autumn can attract crowds of colourful migratory butterflies, especially Common Tigers. From here there is a concrete footpath through the marshy fields, back to the village.

Alternatively turn left – east – at the beach, and there is a campsite above the

Upper Cheung Sha can be a place for fishing...

for swimming and bodyboarding ...

Pui O attracts migrants like tiger butterflies ...

and birds including Brown Shrike

and for simply chilling out, enjoying magic hour at dusk

tideline. Further east, beyond a stream mouth, you can paddle across at low tide. A quiet road leads over hills to Shap Long, where there are also buffalo fields, a stream and a beach. Few people know Shap Long, so it is a good place if you are concerned by cantankerous campers and wish to admire bucolic scenes of buffaloes grazing, perhaps beside trees with autumnal colours.

West of Cheung Sha there is another good beach for swimming at Tong Fuk, and beyond it is a sheltered cove at Shui Hau, where the silty shore teems with marine life. Unless it is high tide, you can search for shellfish, hermit crabs, regular crabs and horseshoe crabs – which are 'living fossils' that indeed look as though they are from a long-lost era.

The shellfish may attract some wading birds, but also people, many of whom arrive to collect shellfish, which seems like a recent fashion for city people and has lead to over-harvesting.

Shui Hau can be peaceful, too, and is especially sublime at sunset on a fine day.

Shui Hau tidal flats and mangroves

Cattle Egrets and Water Buffalo

Mui Wo, aka Silvermine Bay, was the main entry point for Lantau until Tung Chung New Town was established. It has a beach – although it does not rival the beaches of the south coast, it is worth a visit, especially for two splendid waterfalls.

Stroll towards the beach, and there is a left turn by a creek lined with mangroves. Turn right alongside the stream, and soon left again, by an impressive old banyan tree. The path leads by old fields with scattered housing, then up through woodland on Butterfly Hill, which is more of a mound than a hill. The path drops to the stream, and after a footbridge there is a turn right towards the main Silvermine Fall. This is a popular place, complete with a viewing pavilion.

To find the second, 'hidden' falls, walk uphill, past the entrance to an abandoned silver mine. The path enters a valley, where you cross a footbridge, head up between small farmhouses, and look for a dirt path at the base of a steep, wooded slope. Follow this and you will arrive at the upper waterfall, which cascades down a rocky slope.

If the flow is not too mighty you can cross it, then scramble up alongside the fall (take care!), to the base of a plunge pool below a short, vertical fall. This is a lovely place, with cascades close by and views out across the wooded valley to the world beyond.

Easily reached, sublime Silvermine Fall

Getting there
- New Lantao Bus Company (http://www.new-lantaobus.com) operates several services on the island. For Cheung Sha or Shui Hau, take bus 1 or 4 from Mui Wo; or bus 11 (to Tai O) from Tung Chung; buses to Ngong Ping also pass them but are a little pricier. All buses to or from Mui Wo pass through Pui O.
- Mui Wo is served by bus 3M from Tung Chung, and ferries operated by New World First Ferry (www.nwff.com.hk).

Notes
- Instead of walking at Mui Wo, you could hire a bicycle from near the pier.
- The Countryside Series map *Lantau & Neighbouring Islands* is useful.

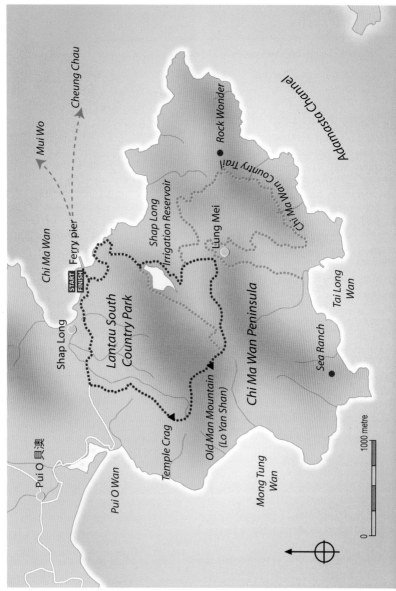

Coast and hills in south-east Lantau

Chi Ma Wan
Forgotten land

9km (5½ miles) ***/****

The Chi Ma Wan (Sesame Bay) Peninsula, south-east Lantau, is easily overlooked, yet can make for a fine day outing.

The peninsula is fashioned from a mass of granite, forming a hilly interior and coastal headlands between small bays. There are few residents, in scattered hamlets and a wannabe fancy housing development. A slender road from Pui O runs across the north of the peninsula, forking to a ferry pier on the east coast, and smaller roads linking two nearby disused prisons.

The Chi Ma Wan Country Trail, at 18.5km (11½ miles) the longest country trail in Hong Kong, starts in the north, and makes a looping circuit above shorelines and up and over the peninsula's highest point, Lo Yan Shan. While it may take eight hours to complete the circuit, there are options for following shorter routes.

If you have never been to this part of Lantau before, it is well worth stopping off at Shap Long, where abandoned fields have become a grassy area grazed by water buffaloes. The area is marred by an ugly new

Looking east from Lo Yan Shan - Old Man Mountain

Clunky name yet serene scene: Shap Long Irrigation Reservoir

development of 'small houses' at the top of the old fields, but is elsewhere rural, with somewhat ramshackle buildings among trees and shrubs by the mouth of a tidal creek.

Follow the coastline south of Shap Long, then head up a rough track, and you arrive at a small reservoir nestled in the hills. It is perhaps only a couple of hundred metres long and is splendidly secluded, with dense woodland fringing the shores. The dam was evidently built to help nearby villagers when they were still farmers, as it is called Shap Long Irrigation Reservoir.

From the dam you can enjoy views of trees and hills reflected in the calm water. The path skirting the north shore heads for a tiny bridge across a stream, in a jungle-like setting, from where you can climb to Lo Yan Shan.

To take a longer route to the hilltop, walk south. The peninsula beyond the reservoir seems remote, the dense woodland often obscuring views of landmarks that might be useful for finding your way. There are occasional trail signs, however, especially at Lung Mei – Dragon Tail.

Though it features on trail signs, Lung Mei is a nondescript place, barely enlivened by a dragon's tail statue resembling a squashed pineapple. It is the prime hub in the Chi Ma Wan trails network.

The country trail passes through here, heading eastwards then south, to make almost a full circuit around a hill. While the trail affords views across the sea to Cheung Chau and passes an area called 'Rock Wonder' – where the hillside is sprinkled

antau's lost world, beside the reservoir

with giant granite boulders – you could readily ignore it if you do not have the time and energy for a full exploration of Chi Ma Wan Peninsula. There is an easy shortcut between Lung Mei and the country trail near the reservoir.

The western section of the country trail almost hugs contours as it passes above the peninsula's south and west coasts.

Another trail drops down to a coastal village, Tai Long Wan. This is one of four places in Hong Kong with a name meaning 'Big Wave Bay', and is a remote village reached only by paths or by sampans from nearby Cheung Chau. Several buildings are deserted, though there is some organic farming and even a Firefly Museum in a village house. There is a fine beach in front of it, and just around a headland to the west lies its bizarre neighbour, Sea Ranch.

Built by the Hutchison group in the late 1970s, Sea Ranch was supposed to become a luxury estate for people wanting to live in a quiet bay beyond the city. But even 'Superman' Li Ka-shing could not lead it to success and it has since languished, with relatively few of the spacious apartments still inhabited. The clubhouse was abandoned; I have seen photos of a long-dead dog on a sofa and a stairway up into shadows, looking creepy as in a horror film. You can, however, readily bypass Sea Ranch, which seems especially wise given that casual visitors are not welcome.

While you can explore the peninsula without getting higher or using more challenging trails than hillside contour ones, doing so means missing out on the best parts: Lo Yan Shan and the nearby craggy hilltop.

There is a trail to Lo Yan Shan from Lung Mei, or you can follow the country trail from the reservoir. There are steep flights of steps, with places where the paths are like corridors between bamboo and trees.

At 303m (985ft), Lo Yan Shan, or Old Man Mountain, is the highest peak on the peninsula. It affords fine views over the sea east of Lantau, with Hei Ling Chau in the foreground and Ping Chau beyond, but it is not the best summit around here.

Walk north, with more downhill stretches and steps uphill, and you arrive at the top of Temple Crag. This is a magnificent place in which to rest and admire the scenery, with Pui O below, the main hills of Lantau soaring beyond it and Cheung Sha beaches to the west.

Not a pineapple, but Lung Mei - Dragon Tail

Getting there

- You can walk to the north of the peninsula from Pui O (served by buses from Mui Wo and Tung Chung), following the road through Ham Tin, then up to the start of the country trail and onwards to Shap Long. New World First Ferry (www.nwff.com.hk) also operates an infrequent ferry service to Chi Ma Wan from Cheung Chau and Mui Wo.

Trail to Lo Yan Shan

Lantau Island viewed from atop Temple Crag

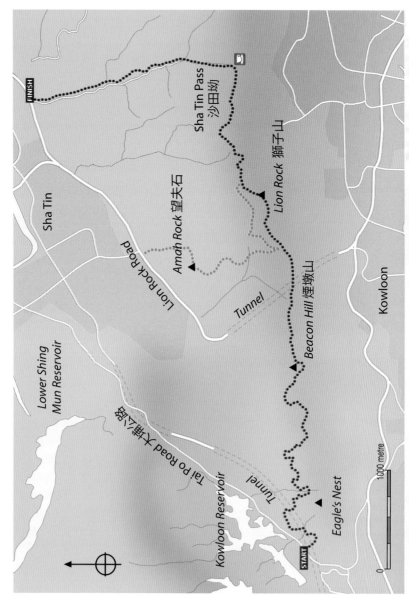

Route featuring Hong Kong's iconic Lion Rock

Over Lion Rock
Spirit in the clouds

10.5km (6½ miles) ****

With the distinctive resting lion profile of the craggy upper slopes, Lion Rock is the most iconic peak in Hong Kong. While reaching the summit takes some effort, the rewards are spectacular views over city and countryside.

The peak is linked to the can-do character of Hong Kong people. This began with a 1970s television series on the lives of working class people, many of whom had lived or still lived in squatter settlements on the slopes below Lion Rock. Later, the Lion Rock Spirit was invoked by businessmen and politicians, and in October 2014, during the Occupy Movement, a band of intrepid activists hung a giant yellow banner on the rock, with black characters proclaiming (in Chinese), 'I want real universal suffrage'.

The precipitous southern slopes of Lion Rock

Soon after leaving the Tai Po Road there is a sign by the path stating: 'Warning – do not feed the monkeys. They may attack you and transmit infectious diseases.' The message is reinforced by a photo of a fierce-looking macaque.

There is a left turn, along stage five of the Maclehose Trail, which here shares the same route as the Eagle's Nest Nature Trail. Macaques are indeed common here. One morning I saw a tree sway and watched as a macaque fed on berries, while almost missing one that was much closer

and drinking from the stream beside me. Another came down to drink; between sips it looked nervously about, as if there might still be tigers or leopards here.

The path winds up the hillside, then levels off, to run through a fine mix of bamboo stands and young subtropical forest. The sounds of traffic fade, perhaps lost in the all-enveloping buzzing of cicadas. There may be more macaques, all well used to people and paying little attention to passing hikers – though do not pull out food if they might spot you.

So close as the crow flies, yet it's quite a trek to the top (foot of trail nearer Sha Tin Pass)

Take care above the cliffs!

A short flight of steps leads to a ridge. The nature trail bears right. The Maclehose Trail turns left, up Beacon Hill.

The uphill path soon leaves the woodland; shrubs grow on the exposed upper slopes. Behind is the hill known as Eagle's Nest, where Black Kites rather than eagles breed.

During the reign of Emperor K'ang-

Hsi (1661–1722), a lookout post was established on the summit of Beacon Hill, with a beacon that was to be lit if attacking ships were sighted. Today there is a radar station on the summit, with the dish enclosed in a white globe.

From Beacon Hill the path runs down, then along the ridge towards Lion Rock, which appears as a sharp cone quite unlike the typical resting lion profile seen from below. There is a lookout pavilion at a junction, with paths leading down and north towards Amah Rock, and down and south to Wong Tau Han in Kowloon. Then there is another junction, where the Maclehose Trail curves away around the north slopes of Lion Rock, and a rough trail heads for the summit, 400m (1,310ft) distant.

The Lion Rock trail proves a tough 400m. At first there are steps, but on reaching the craggy final stretch the steps give out, and in places there is a need to scramble up the rocks. It should be done carefully – a warning sign bears no words, just an illustration of a stick man falling from an overhang.

The trail reaches the high ridge that links three closely spaced summits. There is a fence in front, then empty space, as the sheer south face of Lion Rock drops away. With the cliffs, crags and sharp ridge, this is surely one of the most dramatic peaks in Hong Kong.

Both Kowloon, spread beneath to the south, and Sha Tin, to the north, seem part of a different world. Only a murmur of sound carries from the city. Swifts may swoop around the peak, feeding on insects carried by updraughts.

After clambering up and down the rocky western summit, you can follow the ridge path eastwards. Just before a notice warning of 'danger – steep cliffs', take a path that drops away to the north. It is narrow

Morning mist pouring through the gap between Lion Rock and Beacon Hill

with rough steps, and eventually meets the Maclehose Trail, where there is a right turn towards Sha Tin Pass.

The Maclehose Trail affords easier walking. It does climb before reaching the pass, but does so up the gentle Unicorn Ridge. It passes a few relics of the Gin Drinker's Line – a series of defensive positions was built across these hills in the 1930s to guard against invasion by Japanese forces that were fighting in mainland China. Notions that the holdout might last six months were swiftly proven fanciful in December 1941, when defending troops were forced to abandon the line within just two days. Then there is a downhill stretch, with estates of northern Kowloon close by on the right.

At Sha Tin Pass a shack selling simple food can be a very welcome place for buying drinks on a hot day. There is also a chance to leave the Madehose Trail here, at the boundary of Lion Rock and Ma On Shan Country Parks.

The easiest option is to walk south, down to a bus terminus in Tsz Wan Shan estate, but a path running north is more interesting. It is one of the old footpaths linking the Kowloon area with what is now the New Territories, and follows a stream towards Sha Tin.

At first the stream is small, but with water trickling and flowing in from either side, it soon grows. After a barbecue site a path leads to a pool below a waterfall; this can be an excellent place to bathe in the cool water, and to rest before continuing to Sha Tin.

Kowloon and the hills of Hong Kong Island, viewed from Lion Rock

Amah Rock, standing watch above Sha Tin

Getting there

- To reach the trail leading from Tai Po Road, take a taxi from Kowloon Tong MTR station and get out above Kowloon Reservoir, just after a footbridge.
- From the bottom of the valley from Sha Tin Pass, walk or take a taxi to Sha Tin MTR station.

Notes

- Take plenty to drink: the only place selling drinks (and food) en route is at Sha Tin Pass.
- Be careful on Lion Rock (you could omit the paths to and from the summit by keeping to the Maclehose Trail).
- For an easier, shorter route to Lion Rock, start at Sha Tin Pass – maybe arriving there by taxi. After dropping down to the west, perhaps walk down to Sha Tin via a renowned rock formation, Amah Rock – which, legend has it, is a mother with her child awaiting the return of her husband, but scientifically is a granite tor. Below Amah Rock is a road with bus stops near Tai Wai East Rail station.
- The Countryside Series map *North-East & Central New Territories* is useful.

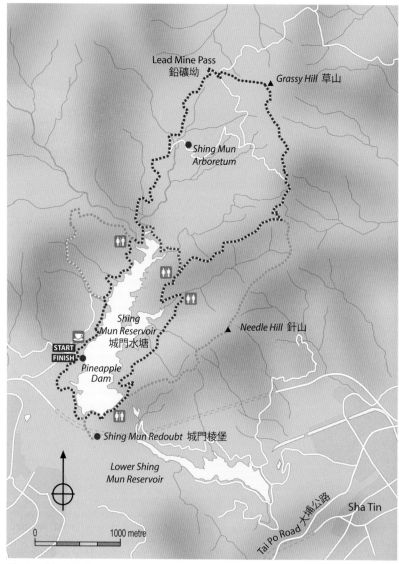

Circuit of Shing Mun Reservoir

Shing Mun

Full circle

8km (5 miles) ***

Enjoy easy strolling through dense forest beside a reservoir set deep in a valley, before climbing a hill and dropping down and round to complete the circuit.

Shing Mun Reservoir at night

After climbing the short flight of steps beside Pineapple Dam, there is a view over the Shing Mun Reservoir, which is typically like a placid lake amid green hills.

A walk along the Pineapple Dam Nature Trail makes for an easy – and pleasant – start to an outing here. It starts at the dam (named after the pineapple groves of drowned villages), passes a picnic site where macaques may linger, and winds north alongside Shing Mun Reservoir.

The trail ends at a service road; a right turn leads further along the reservoir, which is mostly hidden by forest. The road passes through stands of tall paperbark trees, which appear venerable, with grey, peeling bark.

A picnic site among the trees sits on former paddyfields of Cheung Uk Tsuen, one of eight villages whose inhabitants were moved out when the reservoir was built. Below it the Tai Shing Stream empties into the reservoir.

The road crosses the stream, bears sharp left and straightens above another broad stream. At a junction turn left, towards Lead Mine Pass.

A day when it's as if the tide has gone out at Shing Mun Reservoir

The road climbs, though only gently. Damp patches beside it may attract mineral-hungry butterflies, especially large, dark swallowtails that fly up, flashing iridescent blue wing-patches.

There may be macaques, too, seeming wilder and in a more natural home than those that linger near roadsides and car parks. Chestnut Bulbuls are harder to see, but their effervescent calls typically accompany forest walks. These bulbuls only colonized Hong Kong in recent decades or, like the Rhesus Macaque, recolonized. They may have been common here before the original forests were destroyed.

The maturing forest here and in other parts of Hong Kong is allowing some semblance of the area's former wildlife to reclaim the land. For mammals and reptiles, this mostly means an increase in the species that weathered man's onslaught, such as Chinese Pangolins, Masked Palm Civets, Red Muntjac (Barking Deer) and Burmese Pythons. Indian Elephants, South China Tigers and other grand beasts are surely gone for good – the South China Tiger may be extinct in the wild. The Rhesus Macaque, which perhaps also disappeared from the New Territories, was luckier: today's troops may all be descendants of escapees and released animals.

Birds too may escape, find Hong Kong to their liking and breed. Some forest specialists, like the Chestnut Bulbul, might visit and take up residence. While their arrivals are well documented at the Tai Po Kau forest reserve, few birdwatchers bother with Shing Mun. Yet it has a similar mix of birds, and visits can be well rewarded.

Besides aliens such as paperbark trees,

Streams cascade from the surrounding hillsides

Macaques are readily seen around Shing Mun Reservoir

the flora includes interesting native species. Grantham's Camellia, known only from Hong Kong, is found high above the reservoir, and – albeit not growing wild – in the Shing Mun Arboretum, which you can reach by taking a short detour along a road to the right.

Set on 4ha (10 acres) of abandoned fields, the arboretum chiefly grows plants from Hong Kong and South China. Planting began in the early 1970s, and by December 1989 there were 5,070 tree and shrub specimens of 343 species. Along paths signposted, for example, 'Fruit trees, medicinal plants' and 'Plants named after botanists' are 37 species of bamboo, all the Hong Kong camellias and a wide selection of local rarities.

Continue on up to Lead Mine Pass, with its relict name – the mining of lead ore from the nearby hillsides ceased a century or more ago. It lies roughly midway along the old path from Tai Po to Tsuen Wan. Today the main path through here is the Maclehose Trail, which dips down from the east, then climbs westwards to Tai Mo Shan.

Turning right along the Maclehose Trail you can follow a road, then a rough path up Grassy Hill. This leaves the woods; the upper part of Grassy Hill is aptly named, and even those trees that do grow here may be little more than skeletons – probably victims of fire.

Where the path meets with another restricted road, a short walk leads to the cluster of rocks at the hill's highest point. To the north, beyond Tai Po, is Shenzhen; Kowloon lies to the south. But mostly the view is dominated by hills – Tai Mo Shan, the Pat Sin Leng Range and Needle Hill.

The Maclehose Trail takes the road down

Dusk at the north of the reservoir

from Grassy Hill along a ridge. While it climbs Needle Hill before descending to the reservoir, you can take a shorter, easier route by choosing the second of two roads leading off to the right. This drops to a junction near the reservoir, where you can turn left, through woods sparser than those along the opposite shore.

Just before the reservoir's main dam, the Maclehose Trail leads uphill. You could follow it eastwards, to the Kowloon Reservoirs and beyond. But there is also a chance for a short side excursion to find remnants of Shing Mun Redoubt – a fortification along the Gin Drinker's Line, which was built in the 1930s in the hopes of slowing any invasion by Japanese forces. The line was swiftly breached, though parts survive as some of the best Second World War relics. Near the trail you can find trenches, tunnels, a pillbox

and a command post.

To finish the circuit for this outing, cross the main dam, which looks down along the slender Lower Shing Mun Reservoir, set in a deep gorge. The smaller Pineapple Dam is close by.

Getting there
- To reach Shing Mun Reservoir from Tsuen Wan, take a red taxi or minibus 82 departing Shiu Wo Street, 150m (490ft) south of the MTR station, or (at weekends and on public holidays) minibus 94S from Tsuen Wan Pier. The bus stop is below Pineapple Dam.

Notes
- Take food and plenty to drink: there are no shops along the route.
- The Countryside Series map *North-East & Central New Territories* is useful.

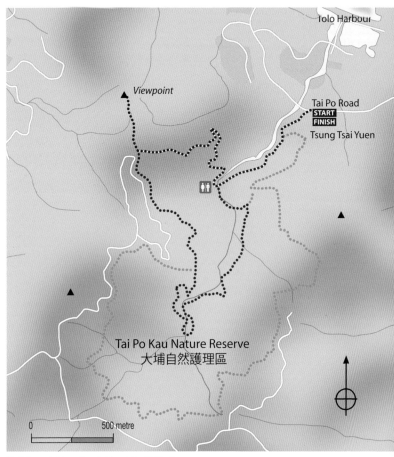

Tolo Harbour

Viewpoint

Tai Po Road
START
FINISH
Tsung Tsai Yuen

Tai Po Kau Nature Reserve
大埔自然護理區

0   500 metre

Trail through Hong Kong's 'Jungle' in Tai Po Kau

Tai Po Kau

There's forest in them thar hills

6.5km (4 miles) *

Take your pick of colour-marked forest trails for a pleasant woodland stroll with a chance of seeing wildlife that includes colourful birds.

Tai Po Kau Nature Reserve is a prime site for birdwatching, along with enjoying subtropical forest and escaping the pell-mell of city life.

The entrance to the reserve is at a lay-by beside the old Tai Po Road. From here, an access road leads into a forested valley.

A couple of hundred metres up the road is the start of a nature trail. This affords a chance to learn of the workings of a tropical forest – of saplings competing for spaces in

the canopy where older trees have fallen, of trees with buttress roots to support them when they are old and huge, and of the sparse undergrowth of a real 'jungle'. If you are not focused on being educated, you can instead walk one or more of the four longer trails through the reserve.

These trails start near a dam, where water from the stream tumbling through the reserve is spirited away to catchment tunnels and reservoirs. Without the forest

Fork-tailed Sunbird feeding on the nectar of a Coral Tree

there might be no water on many days, and mad muddy torrents on others. Without water – or Hong Kong's need for it – there would be no forest.

By the middle of the last century, Hong Kong was largely deforested. As the population – and the territory's thirst – grew, reservoirs were built; above them, swathes of trees were planted to absorb the brunt of rainstorms, and to leak out precious water during dry spells. Many trees were felled during the Japanese occupation, but afterwards tree planting restarted apace. Someone then had the farsighted idea of making Tai Po Kau a special area, with a splendid mix of mostly native trees. Thanks to this mix, the reserve is rich in wildlife. There are civets, Wild Boar, pangolins, and a host of reptiles and amphibians. The Atlas Moth – the world's largest moth by wingspan – lives here. So do birdwing butterflies.

There are plenty of birds, too. Mostly you hear them but do not see them – the ringing koo loo of barbets, effervescent bulbuls, and songs and squawks of laughingthrushes. Even if you cannot place which song is from which species, you can enjoy the sounds of the forest and walk a trail.

After running beside the stream the path turns left and a little uphill. Then you have a choice. There are four marked trails – brown, yellow, blue and red. All loop back to the dam. A map and signpost show the brown and yellow trails heading uphill; they wind around the higher slopes of the reserve.

I prefer the blue and red trails: they are shorter and easier, and pass through the finest forest. Sometimes I combine them, walking part way along the blue trail, then crossing to the red.

The blue and red trails run together for some time. A few minutes' walk leads to a picnic site, where wooden tables with

Morning walkers heading into the forest

benches are arrayed in a grassy clearing. Perhaps because barbecues are banned (lest they ignite the forest), there are rarely more than a handful of people here; often there is no one.

Beyond the clearing the forest becomes dense, with tangled creepers, palms and saplings. Here it is easy to imagine fearsome snakes, like cobras, kraits and constricting pythons, suddenly attacking as they do in B-grade jungle films. They are shy, however, and I have yet to see any in the reserve.

Leaves may rustle as skinks dash for cover. Occasionally on summer visits, non-venomous snakes can be glimpsed. Once a Changeable (or Crested Tree) Lizard waited by the path while I photographed it, then stalked off to find insects in some hidden place.

Another map and signpost mark the place where the red trail crosses the stream and disappears to the right. The blue trail continues, also crosses the stream, almost doubles back on itself, then veers uphill.

The wide, well-kept path levels off. Gaps in the trees afford views across the valley, which is like a green basin on these moist, easternmost slopes of Tai Mo Shan.

Then there are three trails together, as brown and yellow merge from the left. They soon rejoin the access road; the dam is close by. A signpost indicates a path to a viewpoint. Just metres from the road this path leaves the trees. To the north, the slopes are grassy, savaged by fires: they are a desolate reminder of the devastation wrought on Hong Kong's former forests, and of how special this reserve is.

After more steps the path reaches the top of a hill. The promised viewpoint is further on, slightly lower. Among the landmarks, Tai Po and Tolo Harbour are easily recognized; so too are the Pat Sin Leng range beyond Tai Po, and Tai Mo Shan to the west.

Walking along the road again, you come to where the red walk emerges from the trees and the four trails are reunited, before passing the dam and heading down the gentle slope to the lay-by.

Male Changeable Lizard with spring finery

Getting there
- The reserve is conveniently reached by taxi from Tai Po Market station; ensure this takes you to the reserve (stop at Tsang Tsai Yuen), not Tai Po Kau village.

Getting back
- To return to the MTR station, hail a taxi at the main road (you rarely need to wait more than a few minutes for one), or take a minibus or bus to the nearest stop in Tai Po. There are also Kowloon-bound minibuses and buses.

Notes
- Sections of the brown and yellow trails, in particular, can be slippery when wet.
- The trails are clear and well marked, but if you want a map take the Countryside Series map *North East & Central New Territories*.

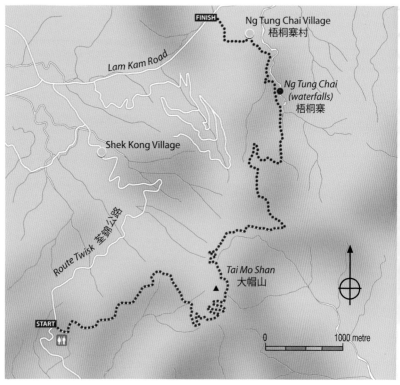

Over Tai Mo Shan, to the Ng Tung Chai Waterfalls

Tai Mo Shan with Ng Tung Chai
Walking in waterfall city
8.5km (5¼ miles) ***

After fine hiking up past Hong Kong's highest summit, drop down through a forested ravine with a series of wonderful waterfalls.

Lantau Island, viewed from Tai Mo Shan

The walk up the road towards Tai Mo Shan from Route Twisk is scenic, with the upper cone of the mountain looming over high valleys and Hong Kong Island away to the south. The view is by no means always idyllic; on still mornings a haze of pallid pollution may hang over the city. However, here you may be above the haze, in cooler, fresher air. There is a barrier that restricts access to the highest stretch of road. Beyond this the road winds up the steeper slopes. Trees are relatively stunted here compared to those at lower elevations, mostly clinging to narrow gullies offering protection from wind and fire, though with others now colonizing formerly grassy slopes.

There are boulders, too – perhaps some are the former travelling stones

that started towards Tsuen Wan, there to improve the *fung shui*, but came to a halt when they were seen by a pregnant woman. Or so the story goes.

The highest accessible point for regular hikers is by the entrance to the wireless station on the summit. Before this was built seasoned hikers reportedly enjoyed the sight of newcomers reaching the top of Tai Mo Shan and tumbling into a concealed hole.

Then down, past an installation where a sign once warned that if you did not stop when challenged, you might be shot. There is a right turn, down a narrow road.

The landscape here seems wild, with rolling green hills ahead and valleys plunging away to left and right. Man helped to shape it, however, felling trees and building the

The Scattered Fall

terraces that pattern the slopes.

At a junction with a map board and signpost there is a trail to the left, towards Ng Tung Chai and the Lam Kam Road. There are stone steps along the footpath dropping downhill, crossing two streams that are typically innocuous but may be dangerous when in flood.

The trail reaches a north-facing spur, with benches for picnickers. Nearby on the left is Kadoorie Farm's eccentric signpost to the world's poles, cities and Wanchai. There are two paths to Lam Kam Road. The one that promises to be most interesting, via Ng Tung Chai Waterfall, is slightly longer. Starting along it, a sign warns 'Difficult terrain: caution'. In early 1995 a landslide blocked a section of this path; though it was then marked 'Road closed', I found that it could be traversed with care. The landslide

debris is, however, unstable, defeating attempts to build a permanent new path.

The trail is easy at first, curving into a valley on the right. Abruptly it enters trees, becoming a woodland path. At this point it is no longer level. Steps lead down the steep slope to the foot of the first of a series of waterfalls. The water spreads into a broad white fan as it descends the Scattered Fall. By the plunge pool is the dark entrance of an abandoned mine. Just below it the trail crosses the stream.

The stream disappears into space. The path leaves it and angles steeply down through a damp world of mossy trees and crags, passing a small stream that plunges over a low cliff to the right. The landslide occurred here; care is needed walking down the rough track over the rocks and stones. The trail angles back towards the first stream, and another waterfall – the Main Fall – comes into view.

A broad column of white drops almost 40m (130ft), ricochets into spray and enters a pool, where on hot days it is refreshing to splash in the cool water. This is one of the largest, most majestic waterfalls in Hong Kong, in a narrow wooded basin that makes a splendid setting.

The path crosses the stream and turns down. The slope is steep here, the trail zigzagging left, right and left again. There is a steep side trail down to another waterfall – the Middle Fall. It is named thus for being between the lower and upper falls, yet perhaps it is also somewhat middling to look at. The stream leaving it is quiet, then surges once more as it drops into a chasm and is lost in darkness.

Follow the main trail down and there is another right turn, to near the stream's exit from the chasm. It cascades out down the Bottom Fall, forms a large, deep pool and

The splendid Main Fall at Ng Tung Chai

Grasses and summer sky, high on Tai Mo Shan

Cascade below the Bottom Fall

Tiny landscape: bryophytes on damp rock

continues, more subdued, through the ravine.

Soon the main path veers away from the stream, and is far gentler. There is a grand temple that can seem remarkably quiet, and not welcoming but somehow almost forbidding. From there the path is concrete, with fields and farmhouses down to the right. There is also the stream, now wide and quiet, the main tributary of the Lam Tsuen River.

At the village of Ng Tung Chai, a left turn leads down a road that wends its way to Lam Kam Road.

Getting there

- You may be able to reach the road barrier on Tai Mo Shan by taking a taxi from Tsuen Wan MTR station (green taxis are cheaper than red ones). Alternatively, bus 51 from Tsuen Wan Ferry to Kam Tin travels via Route Twisk (the road to Tai Mo Shan is on the right as the slope eases, by a sign for Tai Mo Shan Country Park).
- To visit the lower and main falls without crossing the landslide debris, take the hillside path leading down from Tai Mo Shan, then turn right and up the ravine; or walk up from Ng Tung Chai.
- From Ng Tung Chai take minibus 25K, or walk to Lam Kam Road to catch bus 64K or 65K, or a taxi, to Tai Po East Rail station or (perhaps better if you are bound for Hong Kong Island) Kam Sheung Road West Rail station.

Notes

- Take food and drink, since there are no shops en route.
- The path via the waterfalls, especially, may be slippery in wet weather, and impassable if the streams are in flood.
- Ng Tung Chai is covered in two Countryside Series maps: *North-West New Territories* and *North-East & Central New Territories*.

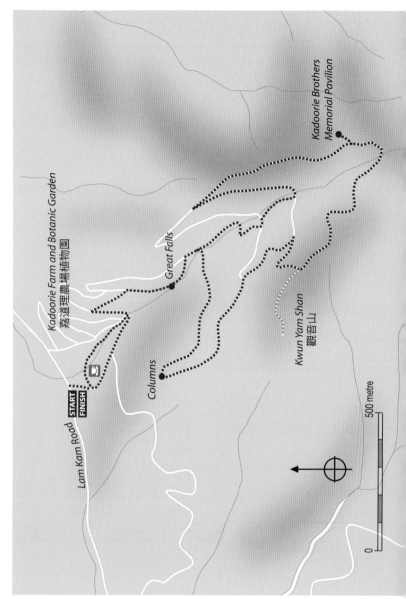

Scenic route through Kadoorie Farm

Kadoorie Farm and Botanic Garden

Eleven miles from Wanchai   6km (3¾ miles) **

Explore an area transformed by farming and conservation efforts, with a waterfall, hilltop lookouts, orchids and other flowers, and wild animals that have been rescued and are being cared for.

Arriving at Kadoorie Farm and Botanic Garden, you can check in at the reception desk and collect a map. Then, for a walk here, start up the road.

The road passes an office, enclosures with animals, and buildings that house an assortment of chickens ('Cocks' summer camp', says a sign). Making the first swing of a zigzag route up the hill, the road turns left and leads through orchards – which flourish in an area 'experts' had declared valueless.

Kadoorie Farm dates back to the 1950s, a time when Hong Kong was recovering from war, its population swollen by refugees from newly communist China. To help refugees and struggling Hong Kong people earn a living, the brothers Horace and Lawrence Kadoorie introduced schemes to benefit farmers. Crucial to their efforts was Kadoorie Farm, established in 1956. It was to be a centre for breeding new crop and livestock varieties, developing new farming techniques and running training courses. That was the idea, anyway. First, the steep, stony hillsides procured from the government had to be planted.

Entrance to the short, shady Fern Walk

North-west Hong Kong, from the Kadoorie Brothers Memorial Pavilion

Brushing aside the doubts of agriculturalists, local villagers set about transforming the area; today, the 'valueless' land, in a steep valley cut into the north of Tai Mo Shan, boasts orchards, woods and gardens. Livestock was reared low in the valley; among it were varieties that, through being better suited to local conditions, have

Hong Kong Birdwing

boosted farmers' livelihoods.

Today there is little emphasis on domestic chickens and pigs. Instead, Kadoorie Farm is also a centre for conservation. Higher in the valley botanic gardens host a mix of foreign and native species – some were first discovered in the valley.

In the lower reaches some animals that were found injured or were illegally traded or brought into Hong Kong are being rehabilitated. Most are in areas that are off-limits to the public. You can, however, visit sanctuaries with owls and birds of prey that are too disabled, or too accustomed to people, to be released into the wild.

The farm also boasts a reptile and amphibian house, a stream-life display, an insect house and a butterfly garden, and houses mammals including Wild Boar and

Leopard Cats.

Where the road makes another hairpin to the left, there is a footpath on the right, signposted to the Great Falls. This path leads to the Lam Tsuen River at the heart of the valley, here fringed with a mix of garden and woodland; the gardeners have been careful to retain original trees and bamboo.

At Great Falls, the river – here just a stream – cascades down a steep rock face; where the spray lands, mosses grow on rocks and trees. A pavilion beside the falls is a secluded place to rest or have a picnic. There is a path that rejoins the road, which follows the stream for a while. Then, as the road bears left once more, there is another chance to walk a path alongside the stream, up past another of the many waterfalls and cascades, which are especially impressive after heavy rains. There are greenhouses here; notices warn that 'Plant thieves will be prosecuted'.

Reaching the road again turn left, walk to

Breed of pig, suiting Hong Kong farms

A Black Kite

a junction, and the road angles sharply to the right by surely the most eccentric signpost you could find on any hillside. Signs radiate from the tall metal post. Each sign has a locality and distance on it and, at the tip, a hand with a finger pointing the way. Neither Shek Kong nor Yuen Long is mentioned. Instead, there are directions and distances for places such as the North Pole (4,665 miles away), the South Pole (7,763 miles), London (5,989 miles), Los Angeles (7,230 miles) and Rio de Janeiro (10,992 miles). Wanchai, to the south, is 11 miles away.

Soon afterwards a left turn takes you to a short diversion to a hilltop vantage point. From the Kadoorie Brothers Memorial Pavilion, you can look down over the valley to the plain, with Shek Kong and, in the distance, Yuen Long. There is a board with a relief map of Hong Kong.

Back at the road continue uphill, then swing around the head of the valley and gently down. In front is craggy Kwun Yam Shan – Goddess of Mercy Mountain. Another diversion heads up towards the 546m (1,790ft) summit, some 400m (1,310ft) above the farm's entrance.

'Hot pots' reads a sign by the summit. This tells of vents that exhale air originating from the foot of the hill, uncooled by altitude. Measurements of the temperatures of

vent air and surrounding air, says the sign, have recorded differences of around six degrees: enough, in cold weather, to lead to mysterious mists around the peak. I have yet to notice even a hint of such vapours here, so believe you need special conditions to see this – and I have put my hand over a vent and noticed no change in temperature, albeit on a summer day, when I did not really want to feel warmer air anyway.

A nearby sign tells of two stone altars: partly because of the hot pots, the hill has long been regarded as sacred. When calamity struck or bountiful harvests were hoped for, worshippers came from the valleys below and prayed to their gods.

Two paths circuit the crag and give fine views. Below, Route Twisk winds its way up Tai Mo Shan, becoming lost from view when it is almost level with Kwun Yam Shan. The upper slopes of Tai Mo Shan are patterned with terraces. A sign suggests that they were created two centuries ago for tea growing, or maybe they are far older and were used for growing crops in times of famine, or by settlers who found no place to live in the valleys.

Heading down you can turn left, to a sharp bend where two pairs of columns might have been props in *Ben Hur*. They are from the previous Hong Kong General Post Office, and were donated by the late Mr Y. C. Liang CBE.

Soon after the bend there is the path past Great Falls, and the road towards reception. After the chicken coops, it is pleasant to walk beside the lower stretch of the stream, where there are more cascades and rock gardens blending planted and wild vegetation. If you did not explore this lower area before, it is well worth checking out the bird and animal enclosures, along with the gardens and greenhouses.

Leopard Cat

Great Falls, with modest flow

Orchids are cultivated and conserved

Reeve's Muntjac - 'Barking Deer'

Getting there

- Kadoorie Farm is open to the public daily except New Year's Day, Lunar New Year (four days), Ching Ming, the Dragon Boat Festival, the Chinese Mid-Autumn Festival (the day after), Chung Yeung and Christmas Day.
- Group visits should be booked in advance – bus routes 64K and 65K terminate at Tai Po East Rail station, with stops on the Lam Kam Road beside the Kadoorie Farm main entrance, or take a taxi from Tai Po East Rail station (to 'Ka Doo Lay Nung Cheung' in Cantonese).

Notes

- There is a shuttle bus along the road up to Kwun Yam Shan, stopping at several interesting sites with a few minutes for each. If you want to explore without walking too much, consider taking this and leaving at an upper stop (inform the driver!), such as the Butterfly Garden, then walk down.
- Maps are available at reception.

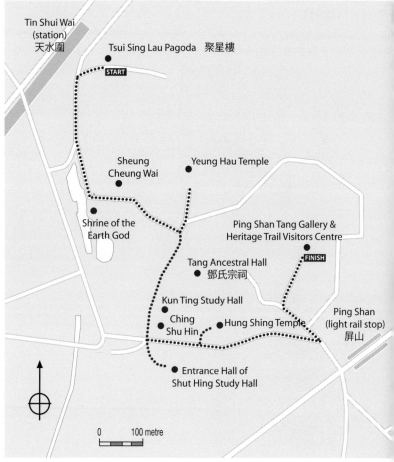

Tin Shui Wai
(station)
天水圍

Tsui Sing Lau Pagoda 聚星樓

START

Sheung
Cheung Wai

Yeung Hau Temple

Shrine of the
Earth God

Ping Shan Tang Gallery &
Heritage Trail Visitors Centre

FINISH

Tang Ancestral Hall
鄧氏宗祠

Kun Ting Study Hall

Ching
Shu Hin

Hung Shing Temple

Ping Shan
(light rail stop)
屏山

Entrance Hall of
Shut Hing Study Hall

0   100 metre

Short trail, long history

Ping Shan
Almost ancient China

4km (2½ miles) *

Follow an easy trail for glimpses of pre-colonial Hong Kong, including temples and impressive ancestral halls.

Tsui Sing Lau Pagoda, Ping Shan

At Ping Shan, beside Tin Shui Wai new town in the north-west New Territories, there is a cluster of fine old buildings, several of which date from well before Hong Kong was claimed as a colony. They are linked by a heritage trail, and include two of the grandest ancestral halls and the only ancient pagoda in Hong Kong.

Ping Shan was reportedly established during the 12th century by a father and son from the Tang Clan. According to the clan genealogy, the pagoda was built around 600 years ago – during the Ming Dynasty.

While subsequent reclamations have led to Ping Shan now seeming well inland, it was then on low hills amid a coastal plain, and the area was susceptible to flooding, especially by typhoon storm surges. The pagoda was built partly to guard against floods by boosting the *fung shui* – and as a sort of grand talisman that would bring local men success in imperial examinations, so they could become officials. Even today, it houses a statue of Fui Shing (Champion Star, or Chief Stars [of the Big Dipper]), venerated as a god of fortune for those taking the examinations.

Though the pagoda was perhaps five or seven storeys tall, today just three storeys remain. The surroundings have been transformed, too; even the fish ponds I visited here in the late 1980s have gone, and the pagoda now faces a car park across a tarmac road, and is backed by the gigantic railway station plus high-rises. It seems a sorry fate for a building that has supposedly stood guard for so long, and at least boosted confidence for students heading for exams.

From the pagoda the trail follows a narrow road, leaving the new town behind. There is little greenery. Rice farming that helped power Ping Shan prosperity stopped decades ago, and today the area is more akin to a scruffy suburb than a proud rural settlement.

There are interesting sights along the heritage trail. A grey brick structure is a shrine to an Earth God, who supposedly protects villagers and maybe resides in a couple of small stones set in an altar.

A newly renovated rectangular building with a doorway and two tiny, arch-shaped windows is the entrance to a walled village, Sheung Cheung Wai. It is flanked by sturdy walls, within which houses are arrayed in tightly packed rows, indicating that former residents must have been willing to sacrifice living space in order to enjoy safety from banditry and the inter-clan battles that afflicted the New Territories.

After a well that might be more than 200 years old, a short footpath leads to Yeung Hau Temple, a simple, squat building with

Ching Shu Hin - a former guesthouse

Entrance to Sheung Cheung Wai

Door gods on guard duty, Yu Kiu Ancestral Hall

Tang Ancestral Hall

Kun Ting Study Hall, where locals once studied for imperial examinations

Hung Shing Temple, dedicated to a deity revered by seafarers

shrines inside, and three openings facing an open-air altar. It is dedicated to Hau Wong, thought to have been a general who died trying to protect two boy emperors as the remnants of the Song court fled Mongol invaders and reached the Pearl River Delta in the 13th century.

The stars of the trail are surely two impressive ancestral halls built side by side and with almost identical designs, like siblings. There is an open area in front of them.

The 700-year-old Tang Ancestral Hall is on the left. As well as having tablets with names of Tang Clan ancestors arrayed in a rear recess, its two spacious courtyards hosted festivals, ceremonies and clan meetings.

Though its neighbour is named the Yu Kiu Ancestral Hall, it too is dedicated to the Tang Clan, and was built by two brothers in the 16th century. It is also more than simply an ancestral hall, and was a school for local children.

Both ancestral halls have traditional Chinese architecture, including roof tiles topped with pottery statues of fish, unicorns and monsters, along with mighty guards painted on their doors.

The Ping Shan villagers were not foolish enough to think a pagoda alone was enough to help pass imperial examinations, and there are two study halls here. The best of them is barely a minute's walk from the ancestral halls. This is Kun Ting Study Hall, and while the exterior looks unprepossessing, inside there is a small, open courtyard plus alcoves with splendidly decorated beams, roofs and door panels. It is relatively new, built in 1870 – just 29 years before the British leased the New Territories, and 35 years before China abolished the imperial

examination system. Even so, it is steeped in the traditions of imperial China. From early last century till soon after the Second World War, local children studied here. Today, the study hall is a restored relic of the past, almost frozen in time like a museum exhibit.

Next door a narrow corridor leads through a circular entrance to Ching Shu Hin, a former guesthouse for scholars and visitors. Here too there are exquisite decorations.

The last stop along the trail has colonial rather than Chinese architecture. It is at the top of the main hill at Ping Shan, where in 1899 – the year the lease on the New Territories began – the government built a police station. The police moved out at around the turn of this century, and the three buildings now house the inelegantly named Ping Shan Tan Clan Gallery cum Heritage Trail Visitor Centre.

The main building in particular is in classic colonial style – squarely built, with open archways flanking corridors on both floors, and walls painted white. Inside the gallery are exhibits with items from Ping Shan, including a very fine tapestry. Photos abound; some portray scenes from only a few decades ago, which appear as if taken in another era.

Getting there
- The pagoda is near Exit E of Tin Shui Wai station; the gallery is a few minutes' walk from the Ping Shan Stop along the Light Rail Transit System.

Notes
- Opening times of buildings vary; they are typically 9 a.m. to 1 p.m., and 2 p.m. to 5 p.m., though the Gallery is open from 9 a.m. to 6 p.m. in summer, closing on Mondays.

Trail through Sha Lo Tung

Sha Lo Tung to Lau Shui Heung

Still wild and tranquil   5.5km (3½ miles) ***

Head up from beside Tai Po Market to roam through a bucolic basin ringed by hills and a valley like a lost world, and pass two small reservoirs.

Trail to Ping Shan Chai, with the Pat Sin Leng range beyond

Though only short, the road to Sha Lo Tung links two very contrasting places – the wealth- and pollution-generating Tai Po Industrial Estate, and a rural backwater that had long seemed destined for transformation so it too would generate wealth, while wrecking a natural gem.

A sign warns that the road is narrow and winding – drivers should take care – and there is a long uphill stretch. A plantation hides the view, and the road emerges on a hillside with scrubland. Then there is a right turn through a gully, and to the road's end at a tiny car park, where there is little more than an emergency phone and an information board that no longer has information.

A concrete footpath runs behind the board, crossing a stream, then leading northwards across still tranquil Sha Lo Tung. Beside it former fields have been recolonized by flowers and shrubs. Groves of imposing bamboo fringe the path. Then the path reaches the open expanse of the Sha Lo Tung basin.

Perhaps always marshy, the basin was home to generations of rice farmers, but in the 1970s city life proved more attractive

Abandoned village amidst resurgent greenery

than rural life, and the paddies fell into disuse. Cocooned in Pat Sin Leng Country Park, Sha Lo Tung looked set to return to a wild state. Until, that is, golf course and housing plans were made public, and Sha Lo Tung became a battleground between conservationists and developers, in a case highlighting the risks of keeping villagers' houses and farmland outside country park boundaries. Though the territory's green groups were heartened when plans for the golf course were withdrawn in 1994, in summer 1995 former residents bulldozed abandoned fields, claiming they would restart farming if development did not begin soon. Vegetation was cleared, with trees bashed down and mud churned, yet neither agriculture nor building ensued.

At least the development plans included the preservation of villages. The terrace of Lei Uk looked ready-made for the museum proposed there; however, it was left to become more dilapidated, and was

Common Blue Jewel

Crimson Dropwing

Cascade by Hok Tau Reservoir

Hiker in the Sha Lo Tung basin

increasingly reclaimed by greenery.

Happily, in 2017, the future for Sha Lo Tung brightened, with plans for a 'land swap' that would allow the developer to create a golf course on a nearby former landfill site, while protecting the basin with its wealth of wildlife, including 76 species of dragonfly – the highest tally of any site in Hong Kong.

The trail drops a little towards Cheung Uk, which nestles beneath a guardian *fung shui* wood where fine trees serve as reminders of forest long gone.

The path bears right at Cheung Uk, then offers a shortcut to Hok Tau Reservoir. Rather than taking this you can walk on between the paddies, cross a low ridge and enter a valley that also has abandoned fields. The valley dwellers must have moved out long ago: there is a *fung shui* wood, though no village, at Ping Shan Chai. Cutting into the steep southern slopes of the Pat Sin Leng range, the valley seems wild and remote, yet is only minutes away from the road at Hok Tau.

The path crosses a stream by a small footbridge, then heads through the wood with its fine old trees. Then there is a path towards Hok Tau Reservoir. After the wood, it

Sun-dappled slopes of the Pat Sin Leng range from near Ping Shan Chai

affords views back up the valley, with the Pat Sin Leng Range soaring above, to the north.

Just before the reservoir there are barbecue sites, and a junction with the Hok Tau Family Trail, which loops around the reservoir. For a slightly longer route to the dam, turn left here. Soon the family trail turns sharp right and down, before crossing two streams flowing into the reservoir. Then it goes up again and right.

The second stream, from Sha Lo Tung, has carved a twisting gorge on its way from the basin; you may hear the water tumbling over cascades that can only be glimpsed through trees.

Approaching the reservoir again, there is a trail towards Lau Shui Heung Reservoir, 2km (¼ mile) or three-quarters of an hour away, according to a signpost; Hok Tau Road is just 15 minutes away.

This new trail, part of the Wilson Trail, first climbs the hillside, taking you away from the woodland of the valley. Opposite, Pat Sin Leng's craggy peaks loom over the Hok Tau Reservoir area.

The trail levels off and curves below hilltops covered in shrubs and grasses. To the north, across a plain and low hills, are the high-rises of downtown Shenzhen.

There is another junction with another family trail – this time a circuit of Lau Shui Heung. To the left this trail runs towards Cloudy Hill, then reaches Bird's Pass before returning to the reservoir. However, there is a shorter option, to the right.

Like Hok Tau, Lau Shui Heung Reservoir is small, set among steep hills with wooded lower slopes. It is peaceful, too: the only building evident here is a country park information hut. Just below is a mix of farms, market gardens and village houses that are inhabited, some of them home to commuters.

Pat Sin Leng range from Hok Tau

Getting there
- From Tai Po Market station, it may be possible to take a taxi to Sha Lo Tung; or take bus 75K to the old Fung Yuen Primary School just before Tai Po Industrial Estate, and walk up the road beside the scrapyard, which turns sharp right, then left and uphill. From Lau Shui Heung Reservoir, walk to the first road junction: here you can catch minibus 52K, or maybe a taxi, to Fanling East Rail station.

Notes
- The trails described are well kept and sign-posted. There are several options for taking a shorter route, such as the path from near Cheung Uk to Hok Tau Reservoir.
- The Countryside Series map *North-East & Central New Territories* is useful.

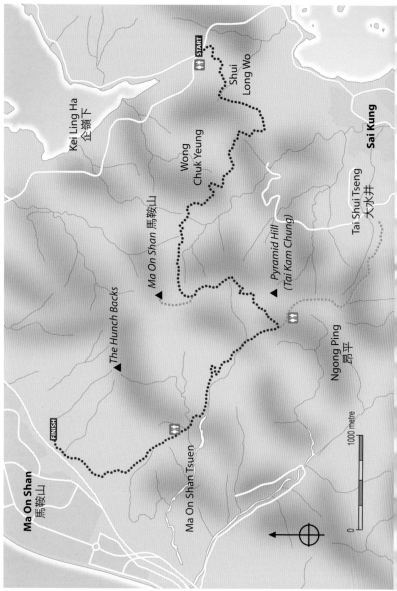

Kei Ling Ha 企嶺下

Wong Chuk Yeung

Shui Long Wo

START

Ma On Shan 馬鞍山 ▲

The Hunch Backs ▲

Pyramid Hill (Tai Kam Chung) ▲

Sai Kung

Tai Shui Tseng 大水井

Ngong Ping 昂平

Ma On Shan Tsuen

FINISH

Ma On Shan 馬鞍山

1000 metre

0

Up and over Ma On Shan, with optional side trail to summit

Ma On Shan
Ascent of Saddleback Mountain

14km (8¾ miles) *****

Hike for the hills to a lofty peak commanding panoramic views, and follow trails through one of Hong Kong's wildest landscapes.

Moments after walking away from the road at Shui Long Wo, a barbecue site is a good place to halt, maybe to smear on sun cream, drink, and eat chocolate or some other food to help fuel the hike. With a stiff climb ahead, this outing is not one to be rushed.

Then, back to the Maclehose Trail. It has just tumbled out of the Sai Kung Peninsula and is now headed for the heart of the New Territories. It is gentle at first, starting along a woodland path, then following a narrow road up through a plantation. The trees thin

out a little; through them there are views over islands dotting Port Shelter. Soon the Maclehose Trail drops down another road, and into a wood with dense groves of bamboo.

Wong Chuk Yeung village nestles in a hollow on the right. There is a right turn onto a footpath, then a sign points left, up steps. The wood is dense here, with trees that are big and old by Hong Kong standards.

The trail is soon twisting right, then left and back again, as it begins the first of three

Craggy summit of Ma On Shan, looking across the Sai Kung Peninsula

main ascents en route to the summit of Ma On Shan. It passes through younger, smaller trees, then shrubs that may be adorned with colourful flowers in spring. The trail arrives at the top of a small ridge that aims for the Ma On Shan massif. Valleys plunge away on either side – out beyond them are Sai Kung town on the left, and Tolo Harbour on the right.

Ahead is the massif's steep, imposing eastern slope, with the Maclehose Trail climbing straight up its middle, and the summit of Ma On Shan to the right, from here looking like a defiant fortress of volcanic rock, guarded by great crags and boulders. Maybe here you can ask yourself whether you are really going up there.

Soon you will reach the end of the ridge and start climbing. The trail is steep, though happily the rough steps are at comfortable heights. As the ridge drops away the view becomes ever more expansive – checking it from time to time makes for a good excuse for occasional halts.

The trail eases, angles up to the left, and enters a dip between two hills to emerge above another steep slope that plunges away to the west. With the second main ascent completed, it is time to sit on the grassy slope and admire the view.

There is a side trail from here to the summit of Ma On Shan. It is steep, rough going, so to be avoided if you do not want to scramble and clamber. The thin path runs away from the Maclehose Trail and up a low hill beyond, which is craggy Ma On Shan.

The path crests the hill, drops slightly to cross a short ridge with steep slopes on either side, then starts up that fortress of volcanic rock. From close up the climb

Spring leaves and flowers, high on Ma On Shan

Highlands of Ma On Shan, looking south over Sai Kung town

South China Barthea

to the very top of Ma On Shan is far less daunting than it appears from below – the path ascends a steep, grassy slope, twisting across and below exposed rock. Even so, you might sometimes use your hands to steady yourself or pull yourself up. Then the path eases and arrives at the level, grassy summit.

What a magnificent place this is! If you are here on a clear day you can see across great swathes of Hong Kong. The lower hills of the Sai Kung Peninsula march away to the east; just visible beyond is the Dapeng Peninsula on the mainland China side of Mirs Bay. To the south are

Getting there

- Shui Long Wo, at the start of the walk, lies along the route of bus 299 between Sai Kung and Sha Tin Central. If you prefer to travel via Sai Kung, take minibus 1A or bus 92 from Choi Hung MTR station, then bus 299 or a taxi.

Getting back

- At the end of the walk your best bet is to take a taxi to Ma On Shan East Rail extension station.

Notes

- Take food and plenty to drink; there are no shops en route. An alternative way down Ngong Ping leads south and down to Tai Shui Tseng near Sai Kung.
- The Countryside Series map *Sai Kung & Clear Water Bay* is useful.

islands, the Clearwater Bay Peninsula and Hong Kong Island – the city is just visible, as is Dragon's Back in the island's south-east. Further away still, almost lost in haze, is Beaufort Island. That is almost the southernmost extent of Hong Kong, while if you take an about turn you can see north beyond Sha Tau Kok to the hills of Shenzhen. To the west is the great cone of Tai Mo Shan; below it, and closer, is Sha Tin.

After admiring arguably the most stunning view in Hong Kong, retrace your steps to the Maclehose Trail. Do this carefully – the path is steep, and hordes of loose stones make it all too easy to slip and fall.

Then continue along the Maclehose Trail. It crests a ridge with yet more superb views, then drops down towards Ngong Ping – an extensive plateau with grassy areas and woodland, which is ringed by hills

Three Fathoms Cove, Sai Kung hills and, in the distance, the Dapeng Peninsula of eastern Shenzhen

Westwards lie Sha Tin and the broad cone of Tai Mo Shan

and seems wild and remote.

Reaching a junction, a right turn leaves the Maclehose Trail. Soon there is an old rural footpath, with solid rock slabs used for steps and a stream burbling cheerfully away on the right.

The path crosses the stream and meets a track running by overgrown mounds of spoil from long-abandoned mines. After an open area the path becomes a road.

There is a small wood close to a ramshackle village on a slope across the valley. The road winds down, levels and crosses a stream near more ramshackle housing. I have seen expensive-looking cars parked here, and imagined the locals up to all sorts of skulduggery far from the watchful eye of the law.

Soon the road passes a large car park near a country park centre, before the rather long and dull, though easy, descent to the edge of Ma On Shan new town.

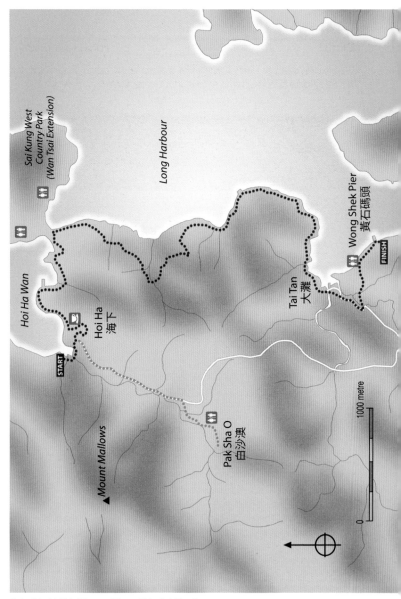

Sai Kung West
Country Park
(Wan Tsai Extension)

Long Harbour

Wong Shek Pier
黃石碼頭

FINISH

Hoi Ha Wan

Hoi Ha
海下

START

Tai Tan
大灘

▲ Mount Mallows

Pak Sha O
白沙澳

1000 metre

0

A stroll by Hoi Ha Wan, and the path to Pak Sha O

Hoi Ha

Hi ho, Hoi Ha

Here is pleasant strolling alongside a bay with corals and other marine life, passing small villages and wooded hills, with a chance for a side trip to a splendid village of traditional Hakka houses.

Hoi Ha village and beach by the mouth of a stream

Though not stunning, the landscape that the minibus from Pak Tam Chung passes through is pleasant and rural. There are hills, fields and woods with old pine trees among a rising tide of deciduous growth. Few buildings are in view. The minibus runs down to Hoi Ha and stops at a small car park.

From here there is a chance to take a side trip, down through remains of woodland – through and past land where a developer plans to build new housing. There is a rough track, a stream crossing where you step between boulders (not to be attempted when the stream is in spate), then a simple path to a small beach beside mangroves – a pleasant place to visit and enjoy the bay, and the stream mouth. From here return to the village.

Here a footpath leads between Spanish-style villas and passes a couple of none-too-fancy restaurants. There is soon a side trail to another beach. Hoi Ha faces out across an inlet (Hoi Ha Wan), towards the mouth of Tolo Harbour. The beach is scenic – a broad arc backed by hills – but hardly idyllic, with drab sand and a dusting of dark silt just below the tideline. Nevertheless, in warm weather people may visit to paddle, swim and picnic.

Beyond this the path turns left, passing older houses and a small temple or ancestral hall. Then it runs through a *fung shui* wood.

Two rebuilt lime kilns are to the right of

Take a deep breath, and just ... relax

the path. First built around 100 years ago, they date to when coral was the basis of a local lime-making industry. Though gone from many parts of Hong Kong, coral is still found at Hoi Ha, mostly fringing the western shore. Nowadays it again helps support a local industry: tourism, albeit on a small scale, and mainly involving day-trippers.

Some 37 of Hong Kong's 50 coral species have been found in the inlet. 'On a calm day,' film-maker Michael Pitts told me, 'you can look down from a boat and see a coral garden. There are brain corals, pinnacle arid plate corals, anemones, tube worms and peacock worms.' However, there are few fish: the area has been overfished, and inevitably, there is pollution – sometimes making the water so murky that visibility drops to little more than a metre.

Fish populations are, however, recovering somewhat, thanks in part to an artificial reef programme by the Agriculture, Fisheries and Conservation Department. 'Reefs' of otherwise unwanted

material like an old ship and clusters of tyres have been sunk in the bay, on patches of bare, muddy seabed. They have attracted fish and become new breeding areas for several species.

While a boat trip is needed to reach the best of the corals, there is a good coral area close to a tiny pier near the path. You can snorkel over the corals, though take care if you enter or leave the water via the rocks lining the shore by the pier.

The path turns a little uphill beside the pier, and runs through scrub, young trees and bamboo thickets.

Soon, on the left, there is a walkway across to a building above the inshore waters, built on stout supports. This is WWF Hong Kong's Marine Life Centre, which also has a glass-bottomed boat to take groups (including schoolchildren) on excursions to view the marine life. The centre and boat proved controversial. Safety concerns helped make the centre costly, and solidly built; it remains off limits o casual visitors, and appears almost orbidding when the gate is locked.

An important step in protecting Hoi Ha came when it was designated a marine park n 1996. Villagers had initially opposed plans for the park, fearing it would mean that they could no longer fish even though they barely do any fishing nowadays. The WWF explained that they could still fish, using hooks and lines, though yes, there would be areas where fishing would be prohibited. 'In New Zealand,' said Ralph Leonard, formerly of the WWF, 'fishermen were first opposed to a similar scheme, but now the area has become a treasure trove of fish.'

Imagine viewing coral and protected fish in Hong Kong. Hopefully more people will have the chance to experience the marine life here, and it will somehow thrive, despite the ongoing pollution. Hong Kong would be a poorer place if the only reminders of its corals were photos, a film and rebuilt lime kilns.

The path reaches the narrow neck of the Wan Tsai Peninsula. This was formerly used as a borrow area – excavating rock for use in construction – but it is tranquil nowadays, with some woodland, and visitor facilities including trails and a campsite.

Turn right here and there is a coastal trail southwards, along a hillside where fires have left little but grass and bare branches. Across Long Harbour is the easternmost part of the Sai Kung peninsula, with the distinctive profile of Sharp Peak. Tap Mun – Grass Island – comes into view a little further south.

The path climbs and runs above a craggy outcrop. Then it rounds a corner, and goes down into a small valley with a small wood and a tiny stream burbling between boulders. It goes up again, left at a junction and on south, beside the inlet.

By the beach north of Hoi Ha village

The path leads across a beach. It keeps low and curves into a bay with mangroves lining the shore. There is a village, Tai Tan, again with Spanish-style villas, at the head of the bay.

At a road you can turn left, to Wong Shek Pier. There is little at the pier – barbecue sites, benches, the Jockey Club Water Sports Centre, vendors selling soft drinks and a bus stop.

For a short bonus trip near Hoi Ha, head to the village of Pak Sha O, the path to which starts about 15 minutes' walk south along the road from Pak Tam Chung. As yet there are no Spanish-style 'villas'; with its traditional houses, it seems almost suspended in time. When you approach on foot trees hide it from view. Pass through these and you will see white-painted houses, mostly arrayed in terraces on gently sloping land.

Explore (quietly!), and you will find grassy gardens, stony ruins adjoining sturdy buildings and renovation work underway. Though it is like a folk museum, there are homes equipped with all mod cons.

Pak Sha O was built by Hakka farmers in

Pak Sha O is a fabulous village

around the mid-19th century. Just two old couples and a man remained by 1985, when the village looked destined to crumble. However, some outsiders arrived to rent places, breathing life back into the village.

The tranquillity may be swept away as a developer has bought parcels of land, and there are plans for hundreds of houses at Pak Sha O and nearby. There is, however, support for conservation. Historian Patrick Hase rates Pak Sha O among the finest villages in the New Territories, and well worth preserving: 'The whole Pak Sha O area is just superb.'

Rebuilt lime kiln at Hoi Ha

Getting there
- You can reach Hoi Ha by taxi from Sai Kung or Pak Tam Chung or – on Sundays and public holidays – minibus 7 from Pak Tam Chung. Bus 94 runs between Sai Kung and Wong Shek Pier (stopping at Pak Tam Chung); on Sundays and public holidays, bus 96R runs between Diamond Hill MTR station and Wong Shek Pier (also stopping at Pak Tam Chung).

Notes
- Hoi Ha has small restaurants; vendors sell drinks at Wong Shek Pier (perhaps only during weekends and holidays).
- The Countryside Series map *Sai Kung & Clear Water Bay* is useful.

Watchtower of the Ho Residence, a Grade 1 Historic Building in Pak Sha O

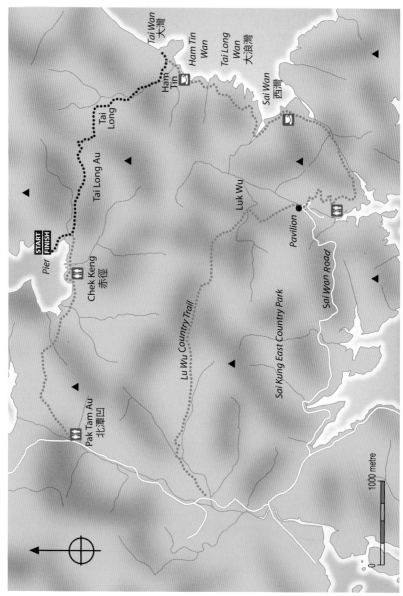

Choices abound for hikers visiting Tai Long Wan, Sai Kung

Chek Keng to Tai Long Wan

Far from the city   7km (4½ miles) to 12km (7½ miles) ***/****

On the east coast of the Sai Kung Peninsula, Tai Long Wan is an expansive bay with perhaps the best scenery in Hong Kong, making a great place for a short hike in summer, or a longer route when the weather is cooler.

If you take the ferry to Chek Keng, you may find that it soon fills up before departing, becoming crowded with rucksack bearers and rucksacks. Passing along Tolo Harbour, the ferry halts at places including Sham Chung and Tap Mun (Grass Island), where groups of rucksack bearers may depart.

From Chek Keng pier walk up the steps and head along the path that leads to the nearby, nearly abandoned village. In spring, you may hear the strident *Brain fever! Brain fever!! Brain fever!!!* song of a Large Hawk-cuckoo from a patch of woodland close by; but you will need luck to see it.

After crossing a bridge over a stream, turn left and go upwards. This is a stretch of Maclehose Trail, and the path will take you to a fine beach. First you must cross the ridge in front. The slope is gentle but persistent. The view changes only a little as

View towards Ham Tin, with the distinctive profile of Sharp Peak beyond

you climb, so it is perhaps a relief to reach the top, in a gap between hills.

This is a good place to rest on the grassy slopes, perhaps enjoying a cool breeze and the view down to the east coast of the Sai Kung Peninsula. While some rucksack bearers may halt, too, most seem compelled to go onwards.

The beach is visible from the slopes, but there is still a way to go. This eastern side of the ridge is steeper, and the path zigzags. On the left rises Sharp Peak, with its distinctive cone-shaped summit; it makes for a good climb, offering outstanding views, but the upper paths are very steep and topped with fine, loose gravel, making the going skiddy underfoot.

Below the hill there is the first village of the day, Tai Long, and the first, basic

Traditional houses at Ham Tin

restaurant, the First Stop. Tai Long is small, a cluster of houses with footpaths for streets. The path runs by another restaurant aimed at hikers and day-trippers, then along the level ground beside a stream.

Soon there are abandoned paddyfields on the left, while on the right a stream flows

Ham Tin's rickety-rackety bridge

Sunrise at Sai Wan

gently towards the sea. Ham Tin lies just around a corner. It is even smaller, though less compact, than Tai Long. Turn off the path to the right, and there is a footbridge over a stream. It is a rickety-rackety-looking bridge, with a skeleton of iron pipes overlaid with a crooked jumble of wood. The unlikely contraption should hold as you cross to the beach, maybe to stroll to the sideline and watch the waves rolling in.

Offshore there are two craggy islets. Look hard and you just may see one or two White-bellied Sea-eagles perched on one of them, showing pale against the dark trees and rock. Inland, Ham Tin is mostly hidden among trees; beyond it rises Sharp Peak and the ridge.

Two restaurants overlook the beach, and while their food may not win fancy gourmet ratings, they afford outstanding views of beach, hills and wave-carved headlands.

Beside the northernmost of them, the Sea View, a short, rough track leads up and over to the superb Tai Wan beach.

Tai Wan beach is around a kilometre long, with no buildings in view. On some days it may be deserted except for a few feral cows. Head north from Tai Wan, follow a trail up and around a hillside, then walk up and through a low gully (there is a small cliff above the shore). You will come to Tung Wan – East Bay – with one of the most secluded beaches in Hong Kong. From here there are rough trails onto the headland bounding the north of Tai Long Wan, and up Sharp Peak.

Especially on a hot day, it may be tempting to simply return home from Ham Tin by walking back over the ridge to Chek Keng – with the path up to the ridge seeming longer going up than it did coming down.

If you have time and energy to spare, there is another part of Tai Long Wan to

Summertime at Sai Wan

discover – across the headland to the south. Walk to the foot of this headland and you can follow the Maclehose Trail up, round and down the blunt headland, to arrive at Sai Wan. Here there is another splendid beach, and Sai Wan village, which seems dedicated to refreshing hikers along with affording opportunities to learn surfing.

There are waterfalls nearby, too, along the Sheung Luk Stream, which you cross just after the headland. Looking at the stream here, it seems to lack the energy for any sort of waterfall; the water above the river mouth may look as calm as a millpond. However, turn up a rough path just over the footbridge and you will soon find the foot

Waterfall and plunge pool along the Sheung Luk Stream, by Sai Wan

distance from the pavilion, then turn right up the Luk Wu Country Trail.

This trail includes a few stretches where you have to climb up flights of steps, but is otherwise gentle and takes you through an expansive landscape that has been all but abandoned by people. The trail crosses Sheung Luk Stream near the long-abandoned village of Luk Wu, where the walls of old buildings are disappearing beneath resurgent vegetation. There is a broad area that is reminiscent of the moors of northern lands, then the trail drops down, to end at Pak Tam Road.

of a ravine, along with cascades through narrow, rocky channels.

A little rock scrambling is needed to reach the first of the main waterfalls, but the effort is well rewarded. The stream plunges into a deep pool formed by an artificial dam – a popular place with daredevils who clamber up a cliff, and jump or dive into the water. Further up are more cascades and waterfalls, though the going gets tougher and ropes may be needed in some places, so it may be best to turn back and make for the village.

Here the restaurants offer what may be the day's last chance to enjoy a meal with a view. The Maclehose Trail passes between the village houses, turning inland, then climbs to a trail junction between two hills. Keep straight on from this if you want to head towards home – or even hike over hills.

The path winds above an inlet of High Island Reservoir and reaches Sai Wan Road, where there is a pavilion from which it might be possible to catch transport to Sai Wan. Otherwise there is a long walk ahead of you, maybe down this road and to Pak Tam Chung.

As an alternative, if conditions are good for hiking you can head west a short

Getting there

- The Tolo Harbour Ferry, operated by Tsui Wah Ferry Service (www.traway.com.hk/渡輪服務), departs the pier at Ma Liu Shui (10–15 minutes walk from the University station).
- You could also hike there along the Maclehose Trail from Pak Tam Chung, which is on the route of buses to Wong Shek Pier: bus 94 from Sai Kung and, on Sundays and public holidays, bus 96R from Diamond Hill station.
- From the pavilion above Sai Wan there is a minibus service to Sai Kung, though there may be only two afternoon departures. On Sundays and public holidays you may find taxis along this road. From Pak Tam Road, at the end of the Luk Wu Country Trail, you can catch a bus to Sai Kung or (on Sundays and public holidays) Diamond Hill or Choi Hung MTR stations.

Notes

- If you plan to hike between Chek Keng and the road above Sai Wan, consider covering the route in reverse – arriving above Sai Wan by minibus or taxi from Sai Kung, and ending at Chek Keng or nearby Pak Tam Au, where it is easier to find public transport.
- The Countryside Series map *Sai Kung & Clear Water Bay* is useful.

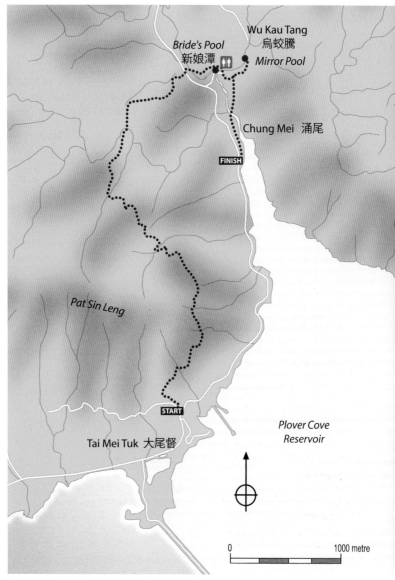

Bride's Pool 新娘潭

Wu Kau Tang 烏蛟騰

Mirror Pool

Chung Mei 涌尾

FINISH

Pat Sin Leng

START

Tai Mei Tuk 大尾督

Plover Cove Reservoir

0   1000 metre

Exploring the Bride's Pool area, near Plover Cove Reservoir

Bride's Pool

A tale of two nature trails

5km (3 miles) ***

Follow a hillside trail above a reservoir to forested ravines with two of Hong Kong's finest waterfalls.

Swirling cascade below Bride's Pool waterfall

Shortly after starting near the Tai Mei Tuk visitor centre, the Pat Sin Leng Nature Trail follows a road and crosses a water culvert. Beside the footbridge is stop one of the trail. It concerns the culvert, which is designed to limit debris entering nearby Plover Cove Reservoir.

The first flight of steps leads up the hillside. One day as I walked here, I heard the cry of a bird of prey and saw a Black Baza cruising past at eye level. The elegant pied bird tumbled down through the air and swooped low over the valley. A second baza joined in the display. Black Bazas were among the birds that colonized Hong Kong as woodland improved, yet for some reason

they seem to have lately declined, albeit they might still nest in the secluded valleys of this north-eastern corner of Hong Kong.

Plover Cove Reservoir dominates the view. Built in the 1960s, it helped put an end to not infrequent drastic water rationing – and was the world's first reservoir built in a marine cove. The idea for it came to T. O. Morgan, the director of Water Supplies, as he swam in the cove east of Tai Po. The initial project was completed in 1968, but the dams were soon raised in another project lasting five years, trebling Hong Kong's water storage.

The path winds in and out of gullies with stands of bamboo. A signpost points to Pat

Sin Leng, half an hour away. It is surely a strenuous half hour, as the nearest peak of the Pat Sin Leng range is 170m (557ft) higher than this junction – so maybe keep to the nature trail.

A craggy bluff hides the reservoir. Eastwards is Wu Kau Tang; the Mirror Pool waterfall pours into the ravine below it. Though more than 1.5km (1 mile) distant, you may hear the surging water. Above and beyond Wu Kau Tang, Mirs Bay is just visible. To the north lies Sha Tau Kok, a town split by the border, and looking more modern and developed on its Chinese side.

The slopes the trail passes are

Getting there
- From Tai Po Market East Rail station, bus 75K runs to Tai Mei Tuk. The start of the Pat Sin Leng Nature Trail is beside the visitor centre, next to the road about half a kilometre east of the village.

Getting back
- From the end of the route walk along the road back to Tai Mei Tuk in order to catch the return bus, perhaps watching for passing taxis. There is also the daily though rather infrequent minibus 20R from Tai Po Market station to Wu Kau Tang, which can stop at Bride's Pool.
- Public transport is better on Sundays and public holidays, when you can also catch bus 275R between Tai Po Market station and Bride's Pool.

Notes
- Take plenty of water or soft drinks: there are no permanent shops along the route, though you can find drinks machines by a car park above Bride's Pool.
- The trails are well marked. The Countryside Series map *North-East & Central New Territories* is useful, and has notes on the nature trails.

uninhabited and mostly covered in dense scrub or young woods. Opposite, there are only patches of woodland, but great expanses of charred hillside or grass where there has been respite from fire for a few months. Though hikers and picnickers pass through here, it seems that they have little impact on the environment compared to villagers who show scant regard for the land in which they live.

The trail starts heading down. It crosses a stream flowing through a narrow, wooded ravine, and there are steps down to the road linking Tai Mei Tuk with Luk Keng, and the end of the trail. Years ago I picked up a booklet on the nature trail, which had a 'note for hearty walkers' pointing out that the Pat Sin Leng and Bride's Pool Nature Trails can be combined. So if you are a hearty walker, you could plan to do just this.

The start of the Bride's Pool trail is just across the road. It crosses a stream,

Mirror Pool waterfall

then leads along the valley side above the waterfall that plunges into the pool. Maybe this is the path from which the legendary bride-to-be fell to her doom when one of the bearers carrying her sedan chair slipped and tipped her down the steep slopes to the stream below.

There is a footbridge across a tributary flowing in from the east. Beside this is a stone tablet, which says the bridge was built in 1906 with donations from Jamaica, Hong Kong, Honolulu and the United States. The chief donor was Sir Cecil Clementi, then District Officer and later Governor of Hong Kong (1925–1930).

A path to the left heads into the ravine from which the tributary emerges. There are steps up, then it becomes a contour path, soon arriving at the Mirror Pool waterfall. At 35m (115ft), this is higher than the Bride's Pool fall. It is more spectacular, too: I once arrived after a long rainy spell, when trees swayed in a wind pushed through the ravine by the foaming torrent. When the fall is quieter you can sit on boulders near the pool, which is said to be used as a mirror by the spirit of the bride, who washes her hair in the stream.

The path is a dead end, so return to the footbridge. From near here you can follow a narrow path up towards the Bride's Pool waterfall. To reach the plunge pool from the end of this path, cross the stream, then walk and scramble upstream. It is a picturesque spot; but again, there is a need to retrace your steps.

Since I picked up the trail booklet the Bride's Pool Nature Trail has been shortened, so nowadays it just drops down a little from the footbridge, crosses another bridge, then climbs to a small car park. For a heartier walk, however, you can keep to the original route. This leads up some steps

Bride's Pool waterfall after summer rains

before continuing down the well-wooded valley towards Plover Cove Reservoir. The stream is mostly hidden by the trees, until the trail drops down and crosses a bridge with fine views of the valley and the water cascading over boulders below.

Another bridge leads over the outflow from a catchment tunnel. The water is quiet as it rushes from the darkness of the tunnel, but when swollen by heavy rains it explodes into roaring whiteness as it crosses a weir below. Then the water becomes quiet in the serene northern bay of Plover Cover Reservoir.

The trail ends at a car park, with the main road past the reservoir nearby.

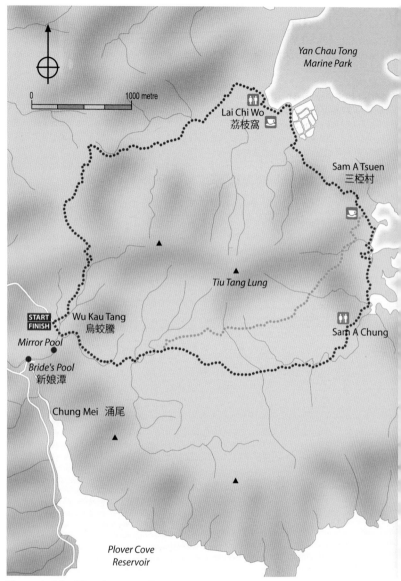

The wonderfully wild north-east New Territories

Wu Kau Tang to Lai Chi Wo
Land of the seven villages

11km (7 miles) ***

After heading to the coast along two scintillating streams, visit old villages, woodland with grand trees and resurgent rice fields.

The hills of the mainland north-east New Territories tumble to the sea, meeting the waters of Mirs Bay along a serrated coastline with a jumble of small stream mouths, inlets, bays and headlands. Rocks, islets and islands are scattered across the inshore waters. A stretch of coast and the nearby shores of the three largest islands encircle a natural harbour known as Double Haven (Yan Chau Tong).

This is one of the loveliest areas in Hong Kong. There are scattered small villages,

most of which are partly or wholly deserted. Much of the coast and the Double Haven islands are within Plover Cove Country Park; Yan Chau Tong Marine Park protects most of Double Haven.

Lai Chi Wo is the main village in this area, and one of seven villages that once formed an alliance called Hing Chun Yeuk. During its heyday it was home to perhaps a hundred households. It is named after the lychee trees the villagers once cultivated, though they switched to more profitable

Old gate to Lai Chi Wo village

Daybreak at Sam A Tsuen

mandarins in the 1960s and '70s. By around the turn of the century, Lai Chi Wo was all but abandoned, with maybe only one family still living here. However, a project to restart rice farming and revive the village is now underway. With several well-maintained buildings including temples, as well as a superb *fung shui* wood and large mangroves, it makes an excellent destination for a hike.

One of the best hiking routes starts at Wu Kau Tang, a village reached by road. From a car park, walk down to an old stone footbridge over a stream. Turn right here, head right again along a thin path through the trees, and you can arrive at the stream above the Mirror Pool waterfall and look down, carefully, to the ravine below. For Lai Chi Wo, turn left after the bridge, skirt the village area and you will soon find a trail to the right.

The path follows the stream, near pools amid dense bamboo. There is a small hamlet, and you head gently uphill. Soon there are marshy patches at the headwaters of the stream. The valley narrows where little but scrub grows on the hillsides, and the path starts descending, gently at first.

Now there is another stream alongside the path, and this is likewise bound for the coast. It is slender, wending through a woodland grove that is the kind of place in which elves might frolic. At a clearing you can walk down to where the stream tilts down a rock slope, with potholes gouged by the swirling flow. It is a top spot to rest before continuing.

From here the trail descends flights of boulder steps. It eases near the mouth of the stream, which is tidal and fringed with mangroves. Though the coast is close by, it is just out of view and you have to walk up through a grassy area to reach the shore of Double Haven.

Double Haven is an area of inshore

waters that is almost surrounded by land – with this coastline to the west, along with islands interspersed with narrow channels. If you ever get a chance to visit one or more of the three main islands, maybe via a boat trip from Ma Liu Shui, they make for a rewarding outing, with an interesting village and fine beaches, along with corals plus colourful fish and other marine life that make snorkelling rewarding.

The trail soon arrives at Sam A Tsuen, with a tidal pool by a hamlet, and a chance to stop for a drink or meal. Then the route turns inland, climbing a little to pass another hamlet, continuing to a gap between hills, then dropping down to the coast again. There is a small headland with purple-red sandstones, and the route turns into the bay at Lai Ch Wo.

Here there is a belt of mangroves, beyond which are mudflats with a bed of seagrass (a kind of flowering plant that can flower underwater). Both mangroves and seagrass are important habitats for marine

The Hollow Tree, Lai Chi Wo

life such as young fish. They also help protect coastlines against storm damage.

Walk north past these mangroves and you will reach a small wood that is like a fragment of primeval forest. The trees

Hamlet at Sam A Tsuen - a marvellous spot to stop for a drink or meal

Streamside tranquillity, along the path from Wu Kau Tang to the coast

Lai Chi Wo villagers once deployed cannons to deter bandits

there are coastal Heritiera, or Looking-glass Mangroves. While Hong Kong's other species of mangrove tree are small, these are big trees with substantial buttress roots for support. The trees are hung with the thick stems of a climber, White-flowered Derris. Some of its stems are 20–30cm (8–12in) across, and the climbers may be more than 100 years old.

The path crosses a small stream, arriving in front of an old school and a temple adjoining a monastery. Nearby are a couple of cannons that are now like antique decorations, but which villagers originally bought with the aim of scaring bandits who sometimes raided Lai Chi Wo.

The village was also walled for protection, with the houses inside laid out in a grid pattern. Though Lai Chi Wo was almost abandoned by the turn of the century, there is a project to revitalize the village; some residents are returning, newcomers are moving in and several buildings have been restored.

The village is on gently sloping land at the foot of hills, and there is a path up the east side to one of the best *fung shui* woods in Hong Kong. More than 100 plant species have been recorded here, and there are some grand old trees. One of these is at the top of the path – it is an autumn maple called the Hollow Tree because its inside has rotted away, leaving an empty space big enough for a person to fit inside. Close by is another autumn maple, which is 23m (75ft) tall, but has become host to a Chinese

Wu Kau Tang; a trail to the coast starts by the lamppost

banyan that is growing in classic strangler fig fashion; its roots may outcompete the maple for nutrients and water, leaving it to die and rot away.

Another large tree, at the south-west corner of the village, was almost killed by humans. This is known as the Five-fingered Camphor, as it formerly had five trunks that grew from ground level. During the Japanese occupation in the 1940s, Japanese soldiers threatened to chop down the whole tree, but villagers rallied to the tree's defence and one trunk was felled instead.

The revitalization project centres on rice farming. Much as at Yi O on Lantau, once-abandoned rice fields have been cleared of wild vegetation, with rice farming restarted – affording a glimpse of the types of scene that were once typical of Hong Kong lowlands. You might visit the new paddyfields, then head back towards Wu Kau Tang.

Rather than retracing your steps, you could use a path up the hills from near the Five-fingered Camphor. It climbs a ridge,

then drops down near a small stream, to end at the village, a short stroll from the car park.

Getting there

• Wu Kau Tang is served by infrequent minibus 20R from Tai Po Market station, or head there by taxi, maybe from Tai Mei Tuk, which is also served by minibus 20C from the station. On Sundays and public holidays take bus 275R from Tai Po Market station to nearby Bride's Pool.

Notes

• If you would like to visit Lai Chi Wo with less hiking, there is a kaito ferry service from Ma Li Shui (near University station) on Sundays and public holidays. The ferry departs Ma Liu Shui at 9 a.m., and leaves Lai Chi Wo at 3.30 p.m. One option could be to take the outwards journey, then hike back.

• At Lai Chi Wo, Sam A Tsuen and Wu Kau Tang, there are small village shops selling drinks and simple dishes like noodles.

• The Countryside Series map *North-East & Central New Territories* is useful.

Further Information – and Conservation

Publications

If you want to continue exploring Hong Kong's byways, you could look at some other guidebooks.

A succession of hiking guides have appeared over the years. They include *The Serious Hiker's Guide to Hong Kong* (FormAsia Books, 2003) and *The Heritage Hiker's Guide to Hong Kong* (FormAsia Books, 2012) by Pete Spurrier, with many photos. As its title suggests, *Above the City: Hiking Hong Kong Island* by Alice Kershaw and Ginger Thrash (Hong Kong University Press, 2005) covers only routes on Hong Kong Island. *Hong Kong Landscapes: Along the MacLehose Trail* by Bernie Owen and Raynor Shaw (The Geotrails Society, 2001) covers the Maclehose Trail, with a focus on the geology en route.

Plants and animals are the focus of *Hong Kong Nature Walks: The New Territories* (Accipiter Press, 2011) and Hong Kong Nature Walks: The New Territories (Accipiter Press, 2012) by David Diskin.

There are also more general books, including titles on identifying local plants and animals. *Birds of Hong Kong and South China* by Clive Viney, Karen Phillipps and Lam Chiu Ying is a good field guide for local birds (Hong Kong Government, 1996); *A Naturalist's Guide to the Birds of Hong Kong* (John Beaufoy Publishing, 2016) is a handy photographic guide by Ray Tipper. The Agriculture and Fisheries Department and Friends of Country Parks have produced a slew of books in the Eye on Nature series. These include guides to wildlife and hiking trails, as well as volumes covering selected country parks, and places such as Tung Ping Chau. Some are Chinese language only, while others may be bilingual, or available in both English and Chinese versions.

Another book by Martin Williams, *Enchanting Hong Kong* (John Beaufoy Publishing, 2013), has articles and photos introducing a host of attractions across Hong Kong, including the countryside.

Most of the major booksellers have Hong Kong sections, though typically without the full range of government publications. Some government publications, notably maps, are available from outlets including Kowloon Central Post Office and the General Post Office, Central.

Websites and apps

You can find information online, including at Martin Williams' site, Hong Kong Outdoors, www.hkoutdoors.com.

The Agriculture, Fisheries and Conservation Department website is somewhat ungainly but has a wealth of information, including on hiking trails: www.afcd.gov.hk/eindex.html; there is also an app, *Enjoy Hiking*. Leaflets on the grandly titled Hong Kong Global Geopark of China – which comprises several areas in eastern Hong Kong – can be downloaded from a related site: www.geopark.gov.hk/en_s5a.htm. The Hong Kong Tourism Board is a useful source of information on various sites of interest: www.discoverhongkong.com/eng/index.jsp; and the *South China Morning Post* website features an expanding collection of articles, photos and videos on local travel (several by this author): www.scmp.com.

The Hong Kong Observatory website has already been mentioned, but as weather is so important it merits another note. It is at www.hko.gov.hk/contente.htm, and the related *MyObservatory* app is especially valuable when you are hiking – including for radar imagery that shows locations and movements of rain showers.

The *Hiking Trail HK* app mainly features maps showing a host of trails across Hong Kong. Local transport is covered in apps such as First Ferry, New Lantau Bus and FlyTaxi (for booking taxis).

Several more general apps are also useful. Google *Maps* can be a boon, though note some areas do not have local mobile phone coverage. *Windytv* covers weather, including computer model forecasts, and is especially interesting if typhoons may be developing or approaching. There are also simple apps that help a smartphone function as a compass or a torch, which can be worthwhile at times.

Please support conservation

The countryside – particularly rural places alongside or even surrounded by country parks – is facing intense pressure from development, with some places already impacted and made less appealing to visitors as concrete replaces greenery. Perhaps you can help in some way, maybe simply by joining Facebook groups and pages such as 'Save Our Country Parks', or green groups like WWF Hong Kong and Green Power.

Some Cantonese Words for Hong Kong Explorers

Here is a small selection of Cantonese words and a phrase you may find useful while heading out to explore the wilder side of Hong Kong. Cantonese words are also shown in roman type to give some indication of how to pronounce words, ignoring the six tones of Cantonese. Don't

worry too much about language; English is widely used in Hong Kong, though you will find people who do not speak it but can surely help you – whether you are hungry, thirsty, or wanting to find the way or take transport.

good morning!	jo san! 早晨
mountain	shan 山
go hiking	haang shan 行山
water	shui 水
swimming	jau seui 游水
north	pak 北
south	nam 南
east	tung 東
west	sai 西
rock	shek 岩
bay	wan 灣
island	chau 洲; also dou 島
headland	kok 角
river, stream	ho 河
village	tsuen 村
here	ni dou 呢度
ferry	pier ma tou 碼頭
bus stop	baa si jam 巴士站
I want to get off (the bus)	yau lok mgoi 有落, 唔該
good	hou 好
looks good, beautiful	hou leng 好靚
tasty (food)	hou sik 好食
very hot	hou yit 好熱
raining	lok yu 下雨
wind	fung 風
strong wind	dai fung 大風
typhoon	toi fung 颱風
thank you (and please)	mgoi 唔該
one	yat 一
two	yi 二; also leung 兩
three	saam 三
four	sei 四
five	ng 五

six luk 六
seven tsaat 七
eight baat 八
nine gau 九
ten sap 十

Acknowledgements

This is a new version of Hong Kong Pathfinder, with a new publisher. For the first version, I thanked friends including Richard Lewthwaite, Malcolm Goude and Numi Goodyear, who introduced me to many fine places in Hong Kong, and Charles Anderson and Mike Currie of the South China Morning Post, who encouraged me while I was working on the columns. Yka Aaltola made the signpost that featured on the front cover, John Eichelberger sketched the walking figure on the signpost (sadly, I have lost the signpost). Wendy Teasdill drew the original maps, Fabian Pedrazzini, Gloria Baretto and Andrew McAulay kindly checked sections of the text, and Alan Sargent played an essential role as editor.

More recently, thanks also to my wife Maya and son David for joining me on many outings to the Hong Kong countryside. Plus to John Beaufoy for publishing this thoroughly revised and updated version of the Hong Kong TrailFinder; along with thanks to Rosemary Wilkinson for project management, Krystyna Mayer as editor, and William Smuts for drawing the new maps.

About the Author

Soon after obtaining a PhD in physical chemistry from Cambridge University, Martin Williams resolved to pursue conservation – which was closely linked to birdwatching, an obsession since his early teens – and headed to Beidaihe on the north-east coast of China as leader of a team studying autumn bird migration.

After travels in search of birds in Beidaihe and southern China, Williams settled in Hong Kong to work as a freelance writer and photographer. Articles by him have since appeared in publications including *BBC Wildlife*, *Discovery*, *Geo*, *National Wildlife*, *New Scientist*, *Newsweek*, *Pacific Discovery*, *Reader's Digest*, *Action Asia* and *Wildlife Conservation*. He was the chief writer for and a contributing photographer to *The Green Dragon: Hong Kong's Living Environment*, and wrote and photographed *Enchanting Hong Kong*. He was co-producer of *Explore Wild Hong Kong!*, the first documentary on outdoor tourism in Hong Kong.

Martin continued to visit Beidaihe, leading further surveys and birdwatching tours. In Hong Kong, he is active in trying to foster nature tourism and conservation, including through Save Our Country Parks. His plans include further travels from his Cheung Chau base to cover East Asia's wildlife and wild places in words and pictures.

Martin has two websites with articles and photos: DocMartin at www.drmartinwilliams.com, and Hong Kong Outdoors at www.hkoutdoors.com.

Index